THE LITTLE ARK

THE LITTLE
ARK *by* JAN DE HARTOG

Illustrated by JOSEPH LOW

HARPER & BROTHERS, NEW YORK

The names of the characters and the villages are fictitious.

To my friends of the Red Cross in Gorcum.

THE LITTLE ARK

When in the night of January 31st, 1953, a northwesterly hurricane combined with a spring tide broke the dikes of southwest Holland, a tidal wave eighteen feet high swept across the islands, smashing everything in its way. Of the village of Niewerland only a few houses and the church remained standing; in the church tower two children and four animals were hiding who escaped destruction. The children were Jan Brink, aged ten, and Adinda de la Maison Rouge, aged eleven; the animals were a dog, a cat, a rabbit and a cock.

The children were the wards of old Parson Grijpma, who had adopted the boy when his parents were killed by a bomb during the war. After the war he agreed to adopt another little orphan, a girl from Indonesia, whose name had led him to believe that she was of a noble Huguenot family. Only when she arrived did he find out his mistake; she was a spindly half-caste with almond-shaped eyes, a flat nose and two little black plaits sticking out behind big ears. Mrs. Grijpma, after a moment's bewilderment, proceeded to treat Adinda de la Maison Rouge as if she were in fact a Huguenot, straw-blond and peach-cheeked like Jan Brink. She dressed her in pink organdy and put a big pink bow on top of her head, which was replaced by an orange one on royal birthdays. But the children of Niewerland did not join in in the pretense. They followed her in the streets, chanting "Adinda is an ape," and Jan Brink fought for her by throwing his clogs and screaming bad language at the enemy, for which he was unjustly punished afterward.

Jan Brink was an outcast himself because he told lies. They were not the usual kind of child's lies, but vast complicated ones that went on for weeks and always ended in disaster. He had for instance told Hendrik, the apothecary's sixteen-year-old son, that he was the emperor of China, secretly pursued by the Japanese. Hendrik, who was a bit backward, believed him unquestioningly and Jan Brink proceeded to frighten the life out of him by staging nightly prowls along the dike, during which he hissed: "Wait here! There they come!"; then he ran off into the darkness, screamed, threw stones, imitated the death-rattle, poured a bottle of red ink over his hands and staggered back to the trembling half-wit in the moonlight, panting: "I killed two of them, take me home." Hendrik, after a week of nightmares from which he woke up jabbering, finally confessed to his father that Jan Brink was the emperor of China and that together they had killed sixteen Japanese, whose bodies they had thrown into the sea. The father called on Parson Grijpma with blood-shot eyes and a razor strop, but Jan Brink saw him coming and fled to his hide-out, the belfry of the church, where he cowered until dusk. Then Adinda imitated the soft, plaintive call of the bittern, their signal that the coast was clear.

The belfry was their playground, and Parson Grijpma himself had made it so. The church was old, the congregation too small to afford a verger, and he had to ring the bells himself. As the ropes were broken long ago, this meant climbing sixty-nine steps, stopping after each score of them to lean against the wall, his eyes closed, his heart pounding, and then, when he finally arrived in the windy belfry, to lay about him with two hammers until his head reeled with the sound, after which he staggered down, deaf and dizzy. It was only human that as soon as his foster children were big enough, he should send them up into the belfry with a hammer each to call the faithful for him. The ringing of the bells of Niewerland became distinctly more spirited when the children took over; the first Sunday it happened the faithful rushed out of their houses in alarm, thinking the dike was in danger.

Once he had sent the children up there, he could hardly forbid them to go to the belfry during the week to play, as long as they didn't touch the bells. They far preferred the belfry to the sandpit in the parsonage garden, where all they could do was make pies under the stern eyes of Mrs. Grijpma, knitting in the arbor. The belfry became their own little world, for it was unattainable to anybody but themselves. Parson Grijpma had climbed those stairs too often ever to dream of doing so again, and Mrs. Grijpma was afraid of heights, so she never climbed higher than the first spyhole and shouted from there. Another reason why the belfry was a world all of its own was that, seen from up there, the village with its little red roofs, small trees and tiny windows looked like a toy village, peopled with little animals. The harbor, in daily life a noisy basin, full of big ships manned with giants who spat black juice, looked from the belfry like a rectangular puddle in the distance, silver in the sunlight, with small gray and black ships; and the giants looked like ants, crawling to and fro.

They would spend hours leaning out of the arches, looking at the gray mole burrowing in the churchyard that was Papa Donker the gravedigger, the fat mouse on the miniature bicycle pedaling through the streets that was Pieters the policeman, and the beetle pulling a matchbox with a shoveling ant inside that was Farmer Bouma, muck-spreading on his field no bigger than a handkerchief. Still farther away, on the hazy horizon, there were the little mills and the stubby tower of Zurland, and to the right the sea, with occasionally a tiny steamer on it, white and yellow, on its way to the Dutch East Indies.

When they were tired of looking at the toy village and its animals, there were real toys at hand: old empty crates, a stack of hymnbooks, a roll of chicken wire and many mummified bats' corpses, looking like strange dusty fruit. The live bats hung upside down high above the bells and were never disturbed by the ringing. They only came out at night and speckled the floor with their droppings. There were also two old pigeons who soon got used to the children, and were no longer upset by their wild and noisy games.

For another wonderful thing about the belfry was that they could make as much noise as they liked. In the world down below they were forbidden to raise their voices except in song; here the sheer act of screaming was a delight. Jan always lay screaming for at least five minutes when he got up there, underneath the biggest of the bells, because it amplified the sound until his own voice frightened him. Then the actual games would start. They would play at Doctor and Patient, or he would marry her to a broomstick with a hymnbook in his hand, or he would whisper ghoulish stories, trying to frighten her as he had done Hendrik

[4]

the half-wit. But she was not impressed, not even by his most blood-curdling fantasies. Ever since she arrived he had tried in vain to bring her under his spell; he had told her ghost stories in the dark about drowned sailors who sneaked back into the bedrooms of their wives at dead of night, with seaweed in their hair and hollow sockets for eyes, but all she had said was, calmly, "They are called 'hantus.'" When she could not be frightened, he had tried to make her laugh with stories about Mr. Flowerpot and Mr. Flattypuss, two monkeys with bowler hats who rowed up and down the creek in a canoe, very fast, secretly drilling holes in ships to get customers, for they were porthole-builders. But she had not laughed; she had said in her flat little voice, "Monkeys don't wear bowler hats. We had two at home."

He couldn't even make her believe him when they played games. She let herself be pinched, tickled and prodded passively; she waited patiently, holding the broomstick, until the marriage ceremony was over; she let herself be dressed up with a red kerchief around her head and a wooden saber in her hand, and then sat down passively in a crate to let herself be bombarded with hymnbooks, when they played at pirates boarding one another on a tropical sea. He had dressed up two crates as wind-jammers with dust sheets for sails; the game of pirates could have been wonderfully exciting if she hadn't forced him to give all the commands of the enemy as well. He had to call, "Telescopes abreast!" to make her peer through her cupped hands at him; he had to shout, "Fire!" to make her throw a hymnbook, which then came flying at him with a rustling sound and hit his ship with a thud. She would never throw one of her own accord, and when he boarded her, swinging his saber, shouting "Hallelujah!" she put her head down between her knees and let herself be spanked without putting up the shadow of a fight. Only

[5]

when the animals arrived did the game of pirates become really exciting, for he made them her crew.

The first animal they got was Bussy the dog, a mongrel puppy given to them by Hank the blacksmith. They had seen him carrying a sack along the dike, and followed him, fascinated by the squeaking coming out of it. Hank, unnerved by the two solemn children silently trailing him, had looked over his shoulder several times, then shouted, "Ksht! Go home!" but that had just made them stand still. When he turned around again they were still following him, only at a greater distance. At last he stood still at the water's edge, glowered, stooped and picked up a stone, but he didn't throw it. They stood looking at each other for a while, motionless. Then he flung the stone into the sea with an angry gesture and called, "Come here." They did not move. "Come here!" he shouted. "I won't eat you!" As they still didn't move, he asked, "Are you interested in a dog?" Adinda was the first to move. She went slowly toward him and stood still, a yard away, looking at the sack, the bow on her head fluttering in the wind. Then Hank opened the sack, and took out a yelping puppy by its tail. It tried to walk, but its legs were too weak, so it just lay on the cobbles of the dike, panting. "If you like him, you can have him," Hank said. As the children did not answer, he added menacingly, "If you don't, in he goes!" and he gestured with his head toward the sea. Then Adinda went toward the puppy, unsteadily because of the cobbles, and picked it up. It started licking her chin. "Thank you," she said, politely. "All right," Hank said, "but don't say you got him from me." Then he shook the sack and three stones fell out of it. As he marched back to the village, the rolled-up sack under his arm, he never looked round.

Mrs. Grijpma was horrified when they came home with the dog, for she hated all animals except one: a beastly cock, as big as a goose, that was called Prince and spent its time torturing five chickens in a pen in the garden. Even Adinda was afraid of Prince, for whenever anybody entered the pen to feed the hens, Prince glowered at the intruder with a beady gold eye out of the side of his head, his floppy red comb hanging limp over one ear like a pirate's bonnet. Then he ruffled the feathers of his neck and flew at the legs as they entered, hissing and pecking. The only one who could enter the cage without being attacked was Mrs. Grijpma, who talked to him in baby language and let him peck her thumb, saying, "That's right, you spunky little thing. Poor, poor birdie, locked up in a cage instead of carousing in the jungle."

When the children brought in the little dog, she said she would not have it in the house; they could keep it in the garden if they liked, but if it entered the house as much as once she would have it put to sleep. They kept Bussy in the garden for a week, feeding him with milk and bread and scraps from the kitchen, but the silly animal wouldn't stop trying to get into the house as soon as it could walk again, and sat whimpering outside the kitchen door until Mrs. Grijpma ripped it open and screamed, "Go away, dog! Shoosh!" Then Bussy started yapping at Prince, who hurled himself against the chicken wire, screeching with fury, until the feathers flew, and that was the end of Mrs. Grijpma's patience. "Poor little dear," she cried. "His beautiful comb is bleeding. Adinda! Jan! Take the beastly dog out of here! If I set eyes on it again, I'll call the butcher." So they had taken Bussy to the belfry, where he lived quite happily and could occasionally be seen peeping out through an arch as they went to school.

[7]

The second animal to be put in the belfry was Ko, the rabbit. Mrs. Grijpma had kept him for Christmas in a hutch at the bottom of the garden. He was given choice titbits from the kitchen to make him nice and fat, and referred to in the household as "the rabbit." As Christmas drew near, the children had gone to feed him reluctantly, because to them he was not "the rabbit" but "Ko." He was silky-white, had big red eyes and long pink ears, and he could laugh. Two days before Christmas Mrs. Grijpma cried out in alarm in the garden and came running back to the house, calling, "Arnold, Arnold! The rabbit is stolen!" As the bells rang out joyously on Christmas Eve, Ko nearly went out of his mind with fear in his new little crate in the belfry; but he soon got used to it, like Bussy, the pigeons and the bats.

The third to join them was Noisette, the kitten. One morning it was found in a tree outside Mrs. Grijpma's window, squealing. Noisette was black with a white shirt front and a white mustache, and had a short tail that ended in a tight hard curl. Mrs. Grijpma poked at it with a broom, calling for help; Mr. Grijpma ran out of his study without his spectacles, peered up shortsightedly and asked, "What is it this time?" She answered, "A horrible wild cat, chasing the birds!" She managed with her broom to shake the branch to which the kitten was clinging, and with a last violent push, she made it lose its grip and it plummeted into the hen coop. During the five minutes that followed, the hen coop was a witches' cauldron full of shrieks, hisses, squawks, flying feathers, rattling wire; then Mrs. Grijpma threw in a bucket of water. The kitten, that had already looked very small in the tree, now looked so tiny that Prince, with the bully's clarion call of courage, ruffled his feathers and threw himself upon the shivering little creature. Then Adinda tore open the door to the hen coop, kicked Prince in the chest,

[8]

snatched the kitten away, and before Mrs. Grijpma had time to take breath, she had vanished round the corner of the house, her plaits flying. The chickens, cackling idiotically, spilled out of the open gate into the garden where they ran in all directions, their necks stretched out, their silly behinds picked bare by Prince vanishing under the hedge, into the arbor, and into the rose bushes where they stuck, screeching. That night, Adinda was locked up in the broom cupboard without food and Jan sneaked down the stairs to whisper through the keyhole, "I made her a little cage with cotton wool. Do you think she'll catch a cold?" Adinda's flat voice answered calmly, "Go to bed."

Once Noisette had got used to the bells too, and was let out of her cage, the game of pirates became really exciting. Bussy would stand in the bow of Adinda's ship, yapping excitedly at each hymnbook as it came sailing at him. Then he would take a wild jump far off the mark, crash on his chin, yelping, snatch up the hymnbook in his teeth and shake it until the loose leaves flew, fluttered out of the open arches with the wind, and snowed down into the churchyard. Ko would peer over the edge of the crate, his big pink ears pricked up, his red eyes gazing unflinchingly, his pink nose sniffing; when a hymnbook soared with its fluttering leaves, he would flatten his ears like a mule and duck.

Noisette would enter into the game only after the fifth or the sixth round. At first she would sit on the foredeck, feigning indifference, washing herself, to cower only when a hymnbook struck. And then, suddenly, she would go wild and start running round the belfry at top speed, jumping crazily, her tail in the air, and Jan would direct his fire at her because she was a sloop trying to board him. When at last everybody was exhausted, when Bussy lay panting with his tongue out of his

[9]

mouth, when Ko hopped limply across the floor laying little black mines, and Noisette lay among the scattered hymns, thrashing her tail, too tired to go on jumping at the wind-blown leaves, Jan would wipe the sweat off his brow, stagger to the enemy and say, "I accept your surrender." Adinda would raise her head, look at him calmly with her almond-shaped eyes and hand him her handkerchief to blow his nose. Then they would all sit quietly in a little cluster among the hymns and the bats' droppings, and gaze through the arch at the orange sunset over the sea, until a voice from the grave shrieked, "Jan! Adinda! Supper!"

Jan would call down, "Coming!" and they would put the animals to bed: Ko and Noisette each in their own crates, covered with chicken wire, Bussy in Adinda's ship on the rolled-up sail. Then they would go downstairs, the loud clatter of their clogs echoing in the stone well of the tower, and walk hand in hand across the churchyard to the parsonage, where the first birds of evening would be warbling in the elms. Then they would quarrel over the soap at the wash basin in the hall, as they washed their hands for supper. Occasionally Jan would kick Adinda, and Adinda would pinch Jan. Adinda never uttered a sound, but Jan always squealed like a stuck pig. Then Mrs. Grijpma would come out of the dining room, the golden light of the oil lamp behind her making a halo in her fuzzy hair, and she would call, "Children! Stop that at once!"

They would file into the dining room, climb on their high-backed chairs between the two old people, fold their hands and ask the Lord to make them truly thankful for what they were about to receive. During Grace, Mrs. Grijpma usually had stomach rumbles, and after Jan had uttered a strangled "Amen," Adinda would look at him across the table without expression, which would make the laugh come out of his nose. Mrs. Grijpma would say, "Pig! Adinda, give him your handkerchief." Mr. Grijpma would say, with strained gaiety, "Well, dear, what is it today?" and Mrs. Grijpma would answer, "What do you think on a Friday?"

This Friday, like all Fridays, Mr. Grijpma pursed his lips and said, "Pea soup, mm, good." And while his wife ladled out the soup, he continued, "Well, children, if you are good tonight, if there isn't a squeak out of you after bedtime, you may ring the bells tomorrow noon for poor old Jake. Nice and slow. Thank you, Mother." Jan asked, "What did he die of?" Mrs. Grijpma started saying, "Well . . ." and Adinda's flat little voice stated, "Drink." Then there followed one of Mrs. Grijpma's harangues, while everyone ate his soup, head bent, listening to the growing whisper in the elms outside as the night wind started to blow in from the sea.

By the time they went to bed, the whisper in the elms would have grown into a soft foaming, and it would go on growing during the night until it sounded like the surf. Then it would die down again toward daybreak, and as the sparrow families began to rummage under the roof tiles and the first garrulous mother sparrows started twittering in the gutter, the land wind would dispel the fog of the dawn, and the sun would rise behind the poplars and the windmills on the horizon. The children would stir in their beds, dreaming, and a weary gull would come home from the sea, to rest on the back of the rusty weathercock on the steeple, white and wild in the early light.

This Saturday morning, the night wind grew instead of abating. As the children went to school, they were very excited; they skipped along swinging their satchels, shouting in the empty streets that echoed with the wild noise of slamming doors and crashing roof tiles.

The gale grew stronger during the morning, and by the time the school doors opened to let the exultant children out, the wind was ripping twigs off the trees. Jan and Adinda ran hand in hand to the church to be in time for Jake's funeral. Already the hearse was waiting outside, its tasseled hangings blown about, the black plume on the old horse's head askew in the wind. Inside, there was slow organ music, dragging the singsong of the mourners.

As they ran up the steps to the belfry, they had to stoop at the spyholes that faced the sea, for the gale blew through them with such force that they would have been thrown into the well of the tower if it had caught them. In the belfry, every gust turned into a whirlwind, and the gusts were very strong. Overhead sounded the shrill shrieking noise of the weathercock, swinging on its rusty pivot.

The two old pigeons cowered in the far corner, huddled close together. Bussy was blown aside as he came to greet them, and he could wag his tail only sideways. Noisette crouched in her crate; each gust ruffled her fur, showing gray skin underneath. Ko cowered also, his ears laid back, and when the wind whistled through the cracks of his crate, he shut his eyes and wrinkled his nose as if he were smelling something nasty.

The cortege took a long time coming out. When Jan finally saw old Mr. Grijpma appear, his black cloak flying, he called "Yes!" and they squatted underneath a bell each, for the wind was too strong to stand up. Jan had the bass and Adinda the treble, and they made them toll with slow solemn strokes, making quivering rings of sound that were distorted by the wind and blown about the rooftops. After fifty strokes, Jan crawled back to the arch to peer into the churchyard. He saw Mr. Grijpma standing at the grave, his skirts whipped by the wind; the four bearers slowly staggered toward him carrying the coffin, sideways, like a boat tacking into the gale. Jan crept back and went on donging to Adinda's dinging for twenty more strokes; then they stopped and went to the arch together. Bussy wormed himself between them and peered down into the churchyard too, yapping.

The coffin with poor old Jake inside was lowered into the grave and Mr. Grijpma stood holding onto his Bible that fluttered in his hands like a live bird. On calm days, they could hear the mourners singing as the coffin was slowly lowered, now they just saw them open and shut their mouths; they looked as if they were yawning. Then there was a sudden gust and Jake's sister's hat blew away. It sailed high into the air, its thin veil streaming, and was caught in the branches of one of the elms round the parsonage. It must have had pins in it, for Jake's sister's hair was loose now and whipped about her face like a horse's tail. The children laughed and Bussy yapped. Overhead, the weathercock screeched as if in pain.

From where they sat they could see most of the toy village, and that morning it looked very exciting, for things were happening everywhere. From Hank the blacksmith's bedroom two white curtains were fluttering like flags; out of a little square window in the back of the burgomaster's house a long streamer of toilet paper was winding its way round the doctor's poplar; one of the trees in the village square had lost a branch lying across the bandstand with a little crowd around it; Pieters the policeman was keeping them at a distance with his bicycle. There was another little crowd in the dead end of the harbor, waving poles and pushing against Mrs. Ool's tiny houseboat, that had broken a mooring and was blown across the narrow canal. Black smoke was belching from Mrs. Ool's chimney and, as it was flattened by the gale, it made the ship look like a little steamer leaving. They saw Mrs. Ool hang out of a window, waving her arms; then a fat man they couldn't recognize walked gingerly across the gangplank, pulled her out and carried her to the shore, her white petticoat filling out like a parachute. There were only a few fishing smacks in the harbor, the drying nets hanging from their mast tops billowed like cobwebs, and little men were trying to catch them to haul them down. The sea was full of white horses and the breakers that smashed against the dike sent up fans of spray, glistening in the sunlight. In the parsonage garden, Prince was struggling with a hen. The wind blew out his feathers, and suddenly he toppled forward, hen and all. He scurried madly about the pen, chasing the hen, that finally dived into the little round doorway of the chicken house; he flashed after it, his red bonnet flying. Poor old Jake was in his grave now, and the relatives had started throwing clay on the coffin, a spadeful each. Then they turned away and ran, leaning backward, to the vestry where there were coffee and cheese rolls waiting for them. Fons the baker, who in his spare time was an undertaker, rolled up the pall, while Papa Donker held his high hat for him. Then they put the naked bier upside down on top of the cloth and started filling the grave with their spades. The gale whipped the tails of Fons' black coat and made him look like a black beetle spreading its stubby shields to fly.

There was so much to see that they forgot the time, and the gale thundered in the belfry so loudly that they didn't hear Mrs. Grijpma calling. They only saw her as she staggered into the churchyard and peered up at the belfry with one hand at her throat and the other between her thighs. They scurried away from the arch, put Bussy back in Adinda's ship and hurried downstairs, their clogs clattering.

Down below, the wind seemed even wilder. It came round corners with a swoosh and they couldn't help but run as it pushed them. Adinda's bow came loose and she ran faster to catch the pennant flying from the crown of her head. As they stumbled into the dark hall of the parsonage they were breathless, and blind from the metallic sunlight that glinted outside, whetted by the gale. The door slammed behind them, and in the sudden silence plaster rustled somewhere. Mrs. Grijpma's voice called from the dining room: "Children! Do you want to bring the house down on our heads?" The door was opened

[15]

again and the wind threw a handful of gravel onto the tiles as Mr. Grijpma entered stumbling. "Oof!" he said as he shut the door, "poor old Jake was nearly blown straight to heaven." Mrs. Grijpma called, "Arnold!" sharply, and then she clapped her hands. "Children, to table, quick! No monkeying about! The porridge is getting cold."

As they sat down at table, the lamp hung slightly swinging and Jan pointed at it, saying, "Look." Mrs. Grijpma said, "Sssh!" with an involuntary whistle. Adinda looked expressionlessly at Jan, who stopped breathing and turned purple. "All right," said Mr. Grijpma, "say your Grace, children." They closed their eyes and Jan said, "For what we are about to receive . . ." Then Mrs. Grijpma had a stomach rumble. It was a beautiful one, starting like a frog's croak, rising to a coo and ending in a toot. ". . . our . . . our Lord," Jan stammered, "make-us-truly-thankful." The "Amen" came out through his nose. He didn't dare look at Adinda, he just saw her small brown hand appear, holding a handkerchief. "I don't know what is the matter with you children today," Mrs. Grijpma said. "Let's hope it is the gale."

There was too much noise outside for the meal to be natural. The lamp went on swinging and the gusts crashed into the trees like waves breaking, and squalls of rain were blown against the windowpanes, only they weren't rain but bursts of spray from the sea, blown over the dike and the rooftops. "This afternoon nobody is to go to the belfry," Mrs. Grijpma said. "This is the perfect kind of day for polishing the silver. We'll all sit nice and cozy in the kitchen and sing as we polish. Now, how's that?" Jan looked at Adinda, but Mr. Grijpma hastened to say, "Mm, good. Pass me the butter, child."

So, after they had cleared the table and done the washing up, newspapers were spread out on the kitchen table, Mrs. Grijpma made hot cocoa and they polished the silver, singing, "Onward, Christian Soldiers," "Little Cart down Sandy Road," and "All Ye Prisoners, Arise." Mr. Grijpma and Adinda who had the deepest voices sang the melody, and Jan and Mrs. Grijpma the descant, chasing one another into ever higher notes until they shrilled more piercingly than the whistling of the gale in the trees. The gale went on growing all afternoon, the gusts thundered like broadsides of big guns and made the old house shudder. When darkness fell, a ragged dusk of racing clouds, the lamp was lit and the drops of spray that lashed the windows could be seen squiggling down the panes, glistening.

When the silver was done, Mrs. Grijpma decided that they would stay in the kitchen and have a picnic instead of going into the big hollow dining room, which reverberated with the thunder of the gale. She made some more cocoa, and eggs and bacon, and when they were halfway through the meal Jan suddenly said, "We didn't say Grace."

Mr. Grijpma looked alarmed and scratched his head; Mrs. Grijpma said, "That is because it is not a proper meal. This is a picnic."

"But it is food," said Adinda.

"Mm," said Mr. Grijpma. "Well . . ."

"In any case, we are truly thankful," Mrs. Grijpma said cheerfully, "so the spirit is there."

The wind got still worse after darkness. They were just about to start a game of Snakes and Ladders, after Mrs. Grijpma and Adinda had cleared the table, when there was a loud tearing noise outside and the crackle of splintering wood. Mrs. Grijpma clapped her hand to her mouth and Mr. Grijpma hurried to the window. He peered out between his hands and said, "Must be a branch that came off. The trees are very old."

Mrs. Grijpma said in a small voice, "I hope it didn't fall on the hen coop. Did you let the flap down?"

"Of course, dear," Mr. Grijpma said.

Mrs. Grijpma sighed. "A real tempest," she said. "Poor sailors. Well, whose turn is it?"

It was Adinda's. She rattled the dice in her small brown hands and, as she threw them, they flashed in the lamplight.

"Six!" Jan cried. "Down the snake!"

"Lll!" Adinda said, sticking out her tongue at him.

"Children, children!" Mrs. Grijpma cried, as the wind hurled itself against the windowpanes with a rattling crash. "This is a game! If you can't stand losing, you go to bed."

Then the kitchen door opened, letting in a whirlwind that dimmed the lamp and set it smoking, and Pieters the policeman came in, his cap on his ears, the strap round his fat chin, his mustache spangled with drops.

"Good evening, all," he said. "Sorry to intrude, but the burgomaster wants the alarm rung."

Mrs. Grijpma clapped her hand to her mouth once more. The children beamed with excitement.

"Holy Apostles!" Mr. Grijpma said. "What's happening?"

"The harbor master registered the highest-known level of the outside water half an hour ago, and the sea is still rising. So he wants all able-bodied men to come to the dike to put down sandbags. Hank the blacksmith and Fons the baker will drive their lorries on to the dike, and give a bit of light with their headlamps."

"Is there any danger to the village?" Mrs. Grijpma asked. "Will our cellars be flooded?"

"I should think so, ma'am," Pieters said. "High tide is only at midnight and the waves are coming over already. So you'd better move upstairs and put some warm clothes on. And better ring the alarm pretty quickly, Parson."

Mrs. Grijpma called, "Prince! Arnold, we must let Prince out!" The children called, "Should we go now? Should we go now?" Mr. Grijpma stood with his mouth open to speak, but Mrs. Grijpma cried, "No question of it! Arnold, if you let those children go up to the belfry in this weather. . . ."

Then Mr. Grijpma called, "Silence!" with his pulpit voice. "The children will put on warm clothes and go with me to the belfry, so will you, Emma. Whatever happens, up there you'll be safe."

"Not in a hundred thousand years!" Mrs. Grijpma cried. "All you men instantly get into a fuss. We've had many a gale before, Arnold, I don't want those children to catch cold, and I'll certainly not go up those creepy stairs in pitch darkness. You are out of your mind."

Pieters said, soothingly, "I think ma'am is right, Parson. I don't think you need put your family that high. Upstairs will do."

But Mr. Grijpma was adamant. Putting on his cape, he said, "Everyone will do as he is told. Get the children's clothes, Emma. Jan, light the lantern. I'll take them up to the belfry, we'll ring the alarm and then I'll come down and take you up there; if needs be, I'll carry you up."

Mrs. Grijpma shut her eyes and opened her mouth but Mr. Grijpma shouted, "And that's final!" with such authority that she shut her mouth and opened her eyes.

After that, everything happened very quickly. Jan came running with the lantern, Adinda hurriedly put some slices of bread into a newspaper for the animals, Mrs. Grijpma tearfully brought down their mufflers and ice bonnets, and as she hoisted them into their duffel coats, she started to weep. "That'll do, Emma," Mr. Grijpma said sternly. "There's plenty of water outside. Come on, children." He took the lantern from Jan and went to the door. "Arnold!" Mrs. Grijpma cried, quaveringly, "do take care!" Mr. Grijpma said, "Of course, dear. I'll be back in a minute." Then he opened the door. The wind burst in, the lamplight dimmed, and there was a clatter as the Snakes and Ladders board was blown off the table with its counters. "Take them by the hand!" Mrs. Grijpma called, then Mr. Grijpma pulled the door shut.

Outside the wind was so strong that they had to turn their backs to it to breathe. As they stumbled blindly along the wall in the swinging diabolo of the lantern light, the first thing they saw was the white wound of the torn-off branch. They had to wrestle their way through its thicket of twigs to get to the corner. There, in the shelter of the house, Mr. Grijpma took them by the hand. "Hold on!" he shouted, and, taking a deep breath, they set out toward the churchyard.

When they left the shelter of the house, the wind hurled itself upon them with such force that Adinda was blown off her feet and Mr. Grijpma's cloak thrown over his head. They staggered struggling in the darkness, the lantern swinging, their shadows reeling about them. Mr. Grijpma shouted, "Get hold of my leg!" and when Adinda had put her arms around his thigh, he let go of her and loosened the neck of his cloak. It flew away like a giant bat, somersaulting into the darkness.

He took hold of Adinda's hand once more and started pulling them toward the churchyard, leaning against the wind. They heard a loud, regular banging noise ahead of them, and as a whirling gust blew Jan forward with his lantern, they saw in the flash of the light the churchyard gate swing on its hinges, screeching and crashing. Mr. Grijpma stopped; then he pulled them round and they ran, swept by the wind, along the wall of the churchyard toward the road. The wall made a right angle there, and as long as they stooped, they were sheltered from the wind. They stumbled on, stooping, until they reached the open space between the church and the churchyard. The gale shrieked in the railings, from the corner a black flag flapped in the gale. It was Jake's sister's hat, caught on the corner spike, its veil thrashing. Mr. Grijpma shouted, "Take a breath, children! This is the worst bit! Hold on!" and they plunged once more into the fury of the gale.

The narrow gap between the church and the churchyard was indeed the worst bit. The blasts that hit them were so ferocious that Mr. Grijpma staggered backward at each of them. The lantern nearly went out as it was blown horizontally, tearing at Jan's arm. It seemed to take them longer to struggle across to the door than it had taken them to get from the house to the corner. Adinda had to let go of her newspaper and bread; it streaked into the darkness like a gull. As, gasping for breath, they opened their mouths, the wind made hooting noises in them and, although they managed to clench their jaws, their lips remained blown open.

At last they lurched into the shelter of the tower, tumbled onto the steps and sat there panting, dizzy and weak. "Well, children," Mr. Grijpma said finally, "I'm afraid you'll have to go to the belfry without me. I don't think I can manage it. Are you all right?" Jan nodded, snuffling. Adinda held out her handkerchief to him, but the wind whisked it away. Mr. Grijpma took her hand and kissed it, then he patted Jan on the head and got to his feet again. "Well, in you go," he said. "Ring the bells good and loud, as if it were Christmas." Then he opened the door of the tower.

There was a strange, throbbing noise inside, as if they entered a huge organ pipe. "Be careful, my dears," Mr. Grijpma said, "God bless you. I'll be back as soon as I can. Don't come down until I fetch you." Then the organ pipe throbbed with a deep, quivering chord, and he shut the door behind him.

They had been in the tower after dark only once before, on New Year's Eve, to ring in the New Year. That night, only a month ago, it had been very cold and still, their steps had echoed solemnly in the silent tower as they climbed it with the lantern, and when they had finally arrived in the belfry and looked out through the arches, they had seen a hazy blue-white world in the moonlight, underneath a vast black dome ablaze with stars, and the bells had sounded cracked with frost when they had rung them. There had been little golden lights everywhere in the toy village covered with snow and, in the harbor, little ships had squeaked with their hooters, thin and reedy in the stillness. Now the dark tower was alive. It trembled, it shuddered, it booed and moaned, each spyhole hooted a different wailing sound and the stairs glistened with moisture blown in from the sea. They stayed close together, edging along the wall, hand in hand. The lantern flame flickered and made the well of the tower expand and contract as in a dream. When they finally arrived in the belfry, they had to crawl on all fours. The wind screeched through the arches, and the bells that had hung motionless for as long as they had known them now swung and groaned in their yokes. Bussy sat whimpering in a corner, his floppy ears blown about by the wind, and from her crate in the darkness Noisette mewed plaintively, standing up, her pointed ears peeping through the chicken wire. Jan put down the lantern in a sheltered corner and looked for the hammers. When he had found them, they huddled close together underneath the bells and started banging away rapidly until their hearts pounded with fright, so terrifying was the noise of the gale and the groaning bells.

Adinda gave up first. She dropped her hammer and hid her head in her hands. Jan banged feebly three more times; then he bent down and shouted, "What's the matter?" Adinda lifted her face and called back, "Something in my eye!" He took her by the hand and she limped after him as he crawled into the corner near the lantern. She sat down against the wall, her legs flat, and he lifted the lantern to look as she rolled her eyes. "Which one is it?" he shouted. "The right one," she answered, pointing at the left one. As she had lost her handkerchief, Jan didn't know what to do, so he shouted, "Blink!" Adinda sat blinking, until two big tears ran down her flat nose. "That's all right!" Jan shouted. "It's gone! Come and have a look!" He crawled to the arch overlooking the village, and peered over the edge.

In the swirling darkness below, glow worms were crawling: men with lanterns running toward the dike. There were few other lights in the village; the glow worms crawled toward a small piece of the dike which was lit up. On its crown two tiny lorries with pin-point headlamps stood facing each other, and between them, antlike men were scurrying in the feeble light. The sea sent up clouds of steam flattened by the gale as they sprang, and every time they sprang, there was a ripple of water between the two lorries, glistening like the scales of fish. Jan sat staring for a while, but he soon gave up for the salt of the spray swirling about the tower stung his eyes.

[23]

He crawled back to Adinda, and sat down next to her. She huddled shivering in the corner, her hands in her sleeves. Jan looked at the lamp, at her pointed knees, her long feet, then he yawned, shook his head with his eyes closed, and gazed sleepily at the far corner where Bussy was squatting. He called, "Bussy!" and tried to whistle, but his lips were numb. He stuck two fingers in his mouth and tried to whistle on them, although he had never succeeded before; this time he didn't succeed either. He yawned again, a long, wide yawn that brought tears to his eyes, and he put his head on Adinda's shoulder. "I want to go to bed," he said. Adinda said nothing, but he felt her stop breathing; then she yawned too. He felt cold and shivery; so, after thinking about it for a long time, he crawled to Bussy, picked him up, put him under one arm and crawled back on all threes. Bussy stood up on Adinda's lap, his tail between his legs, and started licking her nose. They put him down between them so that only his head peeped out. As Jan still felt chilly and a bit lonely in the weird fluttering light of the lantern, he crawled to Noisette's crate, prized loose the chicken wire, put her under his arm and took her to their corner; then he went to fetch Ko.

Ko took some time to settle down. He struggled at first with the other two, and kicked out with his hind legs, but then he gave up and so they sat, the three animals between them, and went on yawning. Noisette was the only one who yawned with them. She opened her mouth very wide and stuck out a long curling tongue. Bussy wanted to play and started yapping, but Noisette sleepily put one paw between his ears and every time he jerked his head up, her claws came out. Ko just sat, his head between their shoulders, and pricked up first one ear and then the other, tickling them. Jan put his hand on his ears to keep them down. Then he settled once more on Adinda's shoul-

der and looked at the belfry sideways. The bells were still moving, groaning in their yokes. The lantern light flickered, and
every time a squall of spray was whisked through the arches,
Bussy yapped. Adinda's shoulder was small and bony, and he
got so uncomfortable and bored that he sat up again and
stretched out his hand toward the lantern. As he did so, a
shadow fell on the floor; that gave him the idea to make bunnies. Every time he wiggled his fingers, Bussy yapped and he
laughed. Then Bussy got bored with yapping and he got bored
with the bunnies; he yawned again and tried to rest his head on
Adinda's lap. The animals were in the way, so he didn't get
any farther than her chest; he turned his head and looked at
her face from below. She had very big nostrils, and he put up
two fingers toward them; before they got there, Noisette's paw
shot out and scratched him and he cried "Ouch!" He crawled
back stiffly to the arch again and peeped out once more, his
chin on his hands.

There was even less to look at than last time, for one of the
lorries was gone. After long peering, he finally discovered it
lying upside down at the foot of the dike. Every time a cloud of
spray burst and flattened, it reflected the light of the other
lorry for a second before flying inland. He could see a small
band of tiny men carrying sandbags which, as soon as they
were put down, were washed away by the glistening sheet of
water rippling over the dike after each breaker. One of the little
men fell on his back, his feet in the air, and vanished; another
took his place and went on putting down little bags, only to have
them washed away. The spray stung his eyes again, so he
crawled back to the corner where Adinda sat, the animals on her
lap, her black eyes gleaming in the lantern light. On his way, he
picked up a hymnbook and, when he sat down again, he started

feeding its pages to Ko. Ko would eat anything as long as it sounded crisp, but it was difficult to find a crisp leaf in the old mildewed book that had lain in the belfry for years in all weathers. He made paper airplanes out of them, which were whisked off into the night as soon as he threw them, so he changed to paper hats. Neither Bussy nor Noisette would keep them on, only Ko did, after he had made holes in them to let his ears through. Adinda said in her flat little voice, "I'm cold." "Well," he answered, "sit on your legs." But she didn't even try to move. Now she had said that, he felt cold, too, and then an idea came to him. "Let's sit in your boat," he said, for it was standing in the other sheltered corner. This time she tried to move, but she was too stiff, so he put the animals in first; then he helped her to roll over and to get to her knees, and he pulled her as she crawled.

Inside the chest it was lovely and warm. They covered themselves and the animals with the sail, and when that wasn't warm enough, with the newspapers that were in the bottom. The lantern stood outside, its golden light shone in little beams through the holes where knots had been. They snuggled down, the animals between them, and fell asleep with the mousy smell of Ko's fur in their noses, Adinda sucking her thumb and holding her ear with the other hand.

Halfway through the night, Jan half woke up because he thought he heard Mrs. Grijpma calling, "Children, children," far away. The wind howled louder than ever, and there was a great gushing sound as if the sea were very near. "Children!" Mrs. Grijpma's voice cried from the depths of the tower. "Darlings!" Then, there came a sound that made him wake up in terror. A screech, a flapping of wings, and suddenly, with a terrifying scramble of claws and rustle of feathers, something clawed up the side of the crate, teetered on the edge, toppled over and fell in, squirming. It was Prince.

He didn't dare move as he stared at the horrible bird panting in the dark corner, uttering breathless squawks. He waited for Mrs. Grijpma to come, but she didn't. There was a lot of banging downstairs, and then a dull crash that set the tower shuddering.

Prince did not move. He remained crouched in his corner, panting, and Jan stared at him more and more sleepily, until he couldn't keep his eyes open any longer.

He fell asleep again, his nose in Ko's fur.

Prince crowed. He stood on the edge of the chest in the gray light of a stormy dawn and squawked, his neck outstretched, his beak open, his eyes shut. His voice seemed to have cracked overnight; what had once been a clarion call now came out as a croak. The animals stirred and Jan sat up, staring at the bird with fear and loathing.

Prince took a deep breath, lowered his head, uttered another squeak, lost his balance and fell off the chest onto the floor. There he could be heard scrambling around, trying once again to greet the dawn, then the wind caught him. He scurried back and jumped onto the edge, the feathers of his neck disheveled, one of the proud green plumes of his tail askew.

The wind had abated a little. It still howled through the belfry, but the bells swung no more and the turbulent clouds of spray were gone. Adinda was still asleep, her mouth half-open and babyish, her cheek resting on Ko's fur; Noisette was playing with the plait that stuck up. Bussy tried to scramble out of the chest, whimpering. Jan took him by the scruff of his neck and lifted him out. As he peered over the edge, he saw Bussy squat with a concentrated expression on his face, make a puddle, then proudly wag his tail and gallop sideways to one of the arches, his ears flopping. Jan felt like doing the same, so he got out of the chest too, opened his trousers and went to the arch through which Bussy was now peeping. But when he looked outside he forgot what he had planned to do, for they were at sea.

While they had lain asleep in their chest, the old church had cast off as in a fairy tale and sailed into the open. There was water as far as he could see, a gray choppy sea full of white horses. As he looked down, he saw that the water came up to the second spyhole. Then, gazing incredulously at the sea all around, he saw treetops sticking out and bits of roofs.

It took him some time to realize that the church had not moved, but that the sea had. The dike was gone, so were the harbor and the ships. All that was left of the toy village were the roofs of the burgomaster's house and Hank the blacksmith's. All the rest was gone, except the tops of the trees in the market square and, far beyond, Bouma's farm. Of the village of Zurland on the silver horizon only the stubby tower of the church remained; its mills and roofs were gone also. Of the parsonage, nothing was left but the square of trees; in one of them three white hens were roosting.

There were a lot of people straddling the burgomaster's roof: men with bundles and women with babies and children. They sat huddled close together; each wave that broke against the front of the house drenched them with spray. On Hank the blacksmith's roof, there were some people too but not as many.

From his bedroom window stuck a pole with a white flag, fluttering in the wind. As Jan looked, he discovered more people in trees, on jagged tops of broken walls, on telegraph poles even. They were all sitting quite still and made no sound, yet, somewhere, he heard a distant wailing. He ran to the other arch and saw that on the land side much more of the village remained, but the streets were lined by roofs only and the trees had shortened to shrubs. On all the roofs, clusters of people were sitting and there were white flags everywhere. In Queen Street, where the newest houses were, a fishing smack was slowly moving between the rooftops and a small boat was taking people off chimneys and out of the trees, to bring them on board. The wailing came from the roof of the orphanage close behind the church. There were children sitting on the top in their nightshirts, and the old nurse was handing out blankets, that thrashed in the wind. As he ran to the seaward arch, he saw, just below him, wedged in a hole in the church's roof, Mrs. Ool's houseboat bobbing up and down with the waves, lashed by spray. A window was broken, and from it two little curtains were flapping.

He ran back to the chest to call Adinda, forgetting to crawl. The gale caught him halfway and blew him against the wall. He went down on hands and knees and scurried toward the chest. Bussy scampered with him, yapping. "Adinda!" he called. "Come quick! Look, look! The village is gone!" Adinda yawned and stretched, then she sat up, smacking her lips, and asked, yawning, "What did you say?"

"Come! Look, quick! The sea's broken the dike! The village is gone and all the people are sitting on the roofs and there's a boat in Queen Street and the house is gone too and three of the hens are sitting in the tree. . . ." Then he ducked, for Prince had

flown at him with a snarling hiss. Adinda jumped out of the
chest, Ko fell out of her arms as she stumbled, and hopped
round kicking out one hind leg. From the chest came the same
frightening squawking, hissing and spitting that had come
from the hen coop the day the kitten fell in. Noisette shot out,
her teeth bared, her broken tail thick and trembling; Prince
leaped onto the edge and went for her, his wings spread. Bussy
jumped at him, yapping and wagging his tail; Prince jumped
on his back and pecked him ferociously between the ears. Then
Noisette sprang, as if shot by a catapult, and dug her teeth in
the green plumes of his tail. Prince screamed, tried to leap back
onto the edge of the chest, but Noisette held on and they rolled
on the floor, flapping, hissing, clawing, fur and feathers flying.
When finally he tore himself free with a screech like one of his
tortured hens, Noisette went on rolling and clawing, three green
feathers in her mouth. As Prince hopped back onto the edge,
Bussy jumped at him again, but he was far off the mark. His
teeth clicked in the air, he hit his nose on the chest, and scampered away, yelping. From the inside of the chest came a tri-
umphant cock-a-doodle-doo, ending in a squawk.

The fight had been so alarming that for a moment both Jan
and Adinda had forgotten all about the village and the sea. As
they went to the arch to have a look and stared over the edge
at the people on the housetops and the drowning trees, they remained preoccupied with the problem of Prince. What had happened to the toy village was bewildering and fascinating, but
it could not make them forget Prince's menacing presence.
Suddenly their little world was dominated by a tyrant.

"Where is Mother?" Adinda asked.

"I don't know," said Jan. "I heard her come up the stairs

last night, but she must have gone back after she brought Prince."

"Gone back where?" Adinda asked. "I can't see the house."

"I don't know," Jan said. "Perhaps she is sitting on a roof somewhere."

"And where is Father?"

Jan shrugged his shoulders. "He told us to wait here," he said finally, "so he'll probably be coming with a boat."

"I can't see any boat," Adinda said, her lips trembling.

"There is one in Queen Street," said Jan, "picking up people."

But Adinda's eyes filled with tears. "I think everybody is dead," she said, "just like in Porworedjo."

"Where's that?" Jan asked.

"That's where our house was."

"Why was everybody dead?"

"They were deaded by the Liberation soldiers, and the kampong was burned."

"Killed," said Jan, "not deaded."

Adinda said, "Lll!" sticking out her tongue, and then she burst into tears. Jan comforted her by patting her on the back, as if she had swallowed something the wrong way. She looked up and said, sobbing, "Ouch! You're hurting me."

Jan said, "That'll do. There's plenty of water outside," then he crawled to the arch overlooking what had once been the land and watched the toy boat between the little rooftops, his chin on his hands. The orphans huddled on their roof like white mice, and the old nurse had her skirts blown up as she crawled, showing pink bloomers. A patch of sunlight swept glistening over the sea, driven by a huge sailing cloud. Two gulls were blown about the sky, changing from white to dark as they swerved into the shadow. Bussy came to join him, whimpering, and he felt hungry. As the patch of sunlight passed, glistening on the tiles of the church's roof, he stood up, opened his trousers and watched the little golden arc being frayed as it hit the wind. Then he went to the arch that faced the sea, and looked down on Mrs. Ool's houseboat. It hadn't moved, it still lay there jammed in the hole in the roof, slightly tilted, and every wave that smashed against its flat stern tossed a shower of silver over it. There was no other ship in sight between the church and the horizon. Where the dike had been, huge milky breakers foamed and whirled. From the sea, where the harbor had been, he could now see a pole sticking out with a pennant attached to it. It must be the mast of a ship.

He couldn't forget his hunger and he thought how nice it would be if he could get down to Mrs. Ool's houseboat and have a look inside. Once, when Adinda and he had stood looking at the little ship from the quayside, marveling at its tiny neat curtains and its door knocker that was shaped like a dolphin, Mrs. Ool had opened the top half of the door and given them two cookies each from a colored tin with the portrait of the four princesses on its lid. They had seen, through the open door, a doll's kitchen with a little stove and a row of small copper pans, and a cage with a canary in it that sang like a teakettle. In her other hand Mrs. Ool had held a little trumpet, and they had waited for her to blow it; but when he had thanked her politely, she had stuck it in her ear and they had scurried away, giggling.

He went back to Adinda, who had stopped weeping and now sat rubbing her eyes with the backs of her hands. He wanted to ask her to play, but then he thought of Prince, waiting in the chest, and he asked, "What shall we do with him?"

Adinda knew instantly whom he meant. "I don't know," she said. "I wish he would fly away."

"He can't," said Jan. "Mother had his wings clipped after he went to see the neighbors. Shall I kill him?"

"Don't brag," Adinda said.

He laughed condescendingly. "I've killed lots of people," he said. "Hendrik and I caught frogs and blew them up with a straw and then when we jumped on them they plopped."

Adinda's lip began to tremble again. "I'm hungry," she said. "I wish Father would come. Pity I lost the bread. It just flew away, as if somebody had snatched it."

"We killed Japanese, too," Jan said. "We cut their heads off, then we threw their bodies into the sea, and we took their heads to the smokery and hung them among the eels. The next day, they were all brown and shriveled like little dolls' and we hid them in our sponge tins."

Adinda cried, "Stop it!" and Jan was delighted and proud. It was the first time he had made an impression on her.

"I'll hit him with hymnbooks," he said, "and then, when he faints, I'll jump on his head and dead—kill him. We'll give the head to Bussy and the wings to Noisette to gnaw on, and then we'll slit him open and give the grass in his stomach to Ko. I'm sure there is lots of grass in his stomach. We'll eat the eggs."

Adinda put her fingers in her ears.

Jan sat thinking of something to say to her that would make her hide her head between her knees, then he would tickle her under the arms, and they would play like Bussy and Noisette, who were rolling in the far corner, pretending. Ko was making a thorough search of the belfry, sniffing everywhere and sometimes sneezing. He seemed to find something to eat, for occasionally he sat up on his hind legs, munching, his eyes closed. He sniffed round the chest, along the bottom, up the sides, and when he sniffed at one of the holes he jumped backward as if he'd been stung, and Jan saw a yellow beak jab through. He picked up a hymnbook and threw it, but the wind blew it onto the edge of the landward arch, where it lay for a moment, the wind flicking its pages; then it was whisked away. He looked for something heavy to throw, but there were only the hammers. He thought of throwing a hammer, but he was afraid of Prince's anger. He thought of putting the chickenwire on top to keep him in, and then pester him; but he didn't dare go near the chest.

"I'm cold," Adinda said in a small voice.

"Well, let's get into the other boat then."

She crawled to the other boat, sniffing. The wind blew up her skirt; her bloomers were pale blue. When they sat down in the chest, he put his hand under her skirt and stroked her thigh, but she had goose flesh. "Let's make our clogs fight," he said. "You be the Spaniards and I'll be the Dutch. At arms, men! Man the guns! Boom!" and he pushed his straw-lined clog toward her. But she shook her head and sat there, shivering, her arms round her drawn-up knees, her hands in her sleeves, her nose running.

"You look dirty," he said. "Where's your handkerchief?"

"Gone," Adinda said, her face puckering.

"You're covered with snot," he said. "Take a hymn." He tore a page out and handed it to her. She blew her nose in it and tears ran down her face again. "I want to go home," she said.

"And I want to be king and keep a harem," Jan said, repeating a phrase he had heard Fons say to Papa Donker, when they were digging a grave. Papa Donker had said he wanted to be cremated.

"Do you know what a cremated is?" he asked.

Adinda shrugged her shoulders.

"I'll tell you," he said. "That is the French word for nurse. What's a harem?"

Adinda snuffled and put her head on her knees.

"I'll tell you," he said. "It's a carriage shaped like a slice of melon, on four wheels, with gold cushions inside, and little bottles and a little vase for tulips, like Fons' carriage. It is drawn through the desert by two white camels with little boys in red coats on their necks, and in it sits a pirate with a telescope, who is a magician. When he sees anybody coming, he can turn himself into an ostrich. Do you know what an ostrich is?"

Adinda looked up, but she said nothing. She stared at him, her black eyes without expression.

"He's married to a mermaid," Jan said, encouraged. "She's very pretty and she spends all her time combing her hair, and she's got little dwarfs polishing her tail all day, and only when the moon is high and the sea is blue and almost silent like in a shell, she wriggles out to the beach and tries the water with her toes to see if it's cold, and . . ."

"Mermaids don't have toes," Adinda said.

"This one has," Jan said, casually. "She's got little feet sticking out just above her tail. She can pick up handkerchiefs with them like you can, and put them in her mouth."

"There was an old man in the kampong," Adinda said. "He had no arms and he could write in the sand with a stick between his toes. He was deaded too."

"Huh," Jan said. "That's nothing. Do you know that Fons can paint with a brush stuck in his behind?"

"Don't lie," Adinda said, closing her eyes.

"I swear it's true. When the village presented the burgomaster

[36]

with his portrait in a frame, you remember? I was there, with Fons. You remember? The band played, and the burgomaster was standing on the stoop of his house, and then Fons said to Papa Donker, 'Is that what I gave sixpence for? I could have done better myself with a brush stuck in my behind.'"

"I'm hungry," Adinda said, "and I'm terribly cold."

"Don't worry," said Jan. "When the tide comes up Mrs. Ool's houseboat will rise and we'll get in and make a fire and eat bacon and eggs."

"Don't lie," Adinda said mechanically.

"Well, Holy Apostles! Look for yourself, you silly bitch! It's right down there, on the roof."

Adinda's face puckered again and she said, miserably, "They're all dead."

"That'll do," Jan said. "You women instantly get into a fuss. Nobody's dead. They're all sitting on the roofs, picnicking. If they were dead, you would see their bellies floating. You just look out there and tell me if you see any bellies floating."

"They don't float straight away," Adinda said. "One of my little brothers was drowned in the Kali and he took a week to come up and Kromo said they all take a week, little cats, little dogs, little boys—everybody."

"Who's Kromo?" Jan asked.

Adinda looked at him without expression, then she shrugged her shoulders and put her head on her knees again.

Jan sighed and looked over the edge of the chest. He found Ko gazing up at him with his red eyes, sniffing. He lifted him by the ears, put him in the chest, turned him on his back and started tickling his tummy buttons. Ko had two rows of them and when he was tickled there, he squirmed and giggled. This time, he didn't like it. He kicked against Jan's wrist with the sharp claws of his hind legs, swung back on his feet and then he started munching the straw in the clogs. Bussy, who must have seen him go in, yapped and scratched outside, so Jan lifted him in too. He called, "Noisette! Noisette! Pst, Pst, Pst!" and she answered from somewhere, a thin plaintive miaow. Only after he had called three more times, he discovered her high up in the belfry, perched on the yoke of the bells. He went on calling and she lowered herself cautiously. He knew what would happen when she trod gingerly on the top of the treble, and he called, "Don't! Stay where you are!" but already she had slipped, swooped down the slope of the bell and landed slap on the floor, the right way up; but she went on shaking her left front paw as she limped toward them. As soon as Jan could reach her he lifted her into the boat.

Now they were all together again, he became conscious of his hunger once more and he looked around the belfry, his head back, munching a straw. It tasted of nothing but summer.

"Hey," he said. "The pigeons are gone. Adinda!"

When he looked down, he saw her shoulders were heaving again and he felt suddenly afraid, for he had never seen her cry before. Perhaps she was dying.

"Are you still cold?" he asked.

She nodded without showing her face. He took the sail and wrapped it round her legs.

"That better?"

She shook her head. He thought of taking off his coat, and he had to decide what would be worse: that she should die or that he should be cold. He didn't want to decide, so he got out of the boat and crawled back to the landward arch. Everything was as it had been when he last looked, only the orphans now had blankets round them and the boat that had been sailing up

Queen Street was heeling over in the very place where it had been before. He wondered how that could have happened, and an explanation occurred to him. He leaned far out of the arch and looked at the tower. He was right: the water had fallen. He could see the dark mark of where it had been. Perhaps, when the tide was at its lowest, the sea would have drawn back altogether, and they could go down the steps and walk. He looked down the well of the stairs for the first time, and saw Mrs. Grijpma.

He stood staring at her for a moment, petrified; then he ran back to the chest, jumped in and hid his head in Adinda's lap.

Mrs. Grijpma's death saved Adinda's life. Until Jan jumped into the chest and buried his head in her lap, she had been just a little half-caste belonging nowhere, cornered at last by the dark power that had so far overlooked her. When Jan, with his childish mind, had been struck by the possibility that she might be dying, without realizing what it meant, he had been right. She had sat crouched in the corner of the chest, her head on her knees, getting colder and colder, slowly sinking.

Now, suddenly, a little boy ran to her for protection. She didn't know what had terrified him so, but she felt the wave of his fear crash against her and engulf her with a terrible panic, in which she wanted to jump out of the chest and throw herself out of the arch into that darkness, waiting for her. But then the wave receded, broken on an age-old instinct within her; she conquered death by stroking his hair with her small brown hand.

When Jan felt the security of her tenderness envelop him, he burst into tears; wild choking sobs shook his body. He tried to cry, "She is there, she is there," but he couldn't utter the words, only the sounds. She went on stroking his hair steadily, even when he put his arms around her and hurt her with his fear. At last he relaxed, exhausted, and fell asleep.

She sat for hours, his head on her lap, her hand on the nape of his neck, and there were no thoughts within her, only a rising hope, until in the end she sat there proudly, not knowing that the solemn joy within her was happiness. The wind howled through the belfry and whistled through the cracks of the chest. Her body was getting stiff and numb. The animals huddled around her, shivering, and the bells started to creak and groan again. She was overcome by weariness, and several times she nearly fell asleep, but every time she was startled out of her drowsiness by a feeling of urgency, as if the others could only sleep in safety as long as she remained awake.

In the afternoon it started raining. Ice-cold showers were blown horizontally through the belfry in violent gusts, that lashed the bells and set them vibrating. The chest in which the children and the animals were hiding was in the trough of the wind, and the rain drenched them. If only she could chase Prince from the other one, they would be warm and dry, but, as she got up and crawled toward the sheltered corner where his chest was, she wavered as she approached. When finally she got up on her knees and peered inside, she saw the bird glower at her out of the side of his head with a malicious golden eye.

Not knowing what to do next, she crawled to the landward arch and peered out. The sea was gray and full of white caps; the orphans sat close together, pressed against the chimney, their blankets flapping; the old nurse had turned her back to the rain and stretched out her arms around the first few, and so she sat, her head bent, her gray hair fluttering. A little boat from the fishing smack in Queen Street was taking people aboard from a roof near the orphanage; the fishing smack itself was still aground, heeling over between two houses. As she sat looking, a sudden movement caught her eye. The front of the house to which the little boat was moored collapsed on top of it, the roof caved in and sank. The people that were on it became bobbing heads in the water that vanished, one by one.

On the roof next to where the house had been, a man started throwing tiles in the water. She stared at him, her mouth open, until it dawned on her what he was doing. By throwing off the tiles, the wooden roof was bared, and he was making a jagged white patch that grew slowly bigger, using the cross-planks on which the tiles had rested as a foothold. He had just about finished stripping the side of the roof that was turned toward her, when his house collapsed too. The roof flattened out and sank slowly down in the waves, but the half that was wood remained afloat with the man clinging to it, and became a raft. The raft turned and started moving away, until it hit a roof across the street. The man stood up, and started helping people onto his raft.

She looked at the roof of the church; there were several patches of bare wood to be seen where the tiles had been blown off; there too the cross-planks on which they had rested formed a little ladder. She crawled to the arch facing the sea and looked down on Mrs. Ool's houseboat. It was still wedged in the hole in the roof. Many tiles had become dislodged and, there again, the cross-planks formed a little ladder. If she could climb out onto the rooftop and throw off two rows of tiles all the way down, they could get down to the houseboat. But the wind howled, and the rain lashed her face, and she crawled back to the shelter, frightened by the daring of her thoughts.

As she sat looking around the belfry, at a loss, she saw the stack of hymnbooks and thought that they might keep them warm if she spread them open over them. Crawling to the hymnbooks, she passed the hatch to the steps; as she peered over the edge and looked down the well of the tower, she too saw Mrs. Grijpma. After the first cold shock of horror, that wave of panic threatened to overwhelm her once more, but again it was broken on the secret strength within her. She crawled on toward the hymnbooks, took an armful and returned to their chest.

When she had crawled to and fro five times through the wind and the rain, she was so wet and frozen that she gave up and climbed into the chest, shivering. Jan was still asleep and the animals, although awake, were too cold to move. She crouched in her corner again, put his head on her lap, drew the animals close to her and started covering her legs with books. She had brought enough of them to cover them all; they came up to her chest, and by wriggling down cautiously, she could make them come up to her chin. She made a little opening to give Jan some air, then the cold overcame her. She sat there, her teeth chattering, and she couldn't stop them. But as it grew dark, the sleeping bodies underneath the books began to radiate some warmth, until only her face remained frozen, and she fell asleep.

She woke up many times because the rain hurt her face or because somebody moved. The wind went on whistling all night and, in her moments of awareness, she heard tunes in it: dancers shrieking, cymbals clashing, the wild twanging of lutes, slowing down to the soft gonging of a gamelang in the blue darkness,

[43]

the drowsy hum of mosquitoes, and then the thin, transparent strain of a shepherd's flute, lightly trailing her to sleep.

Jan woke her up in a cold blue dawn by shaking her and asking in a hoarse whisper, "Is she still there? Adinda? Is she still there?" The wind was gone; a chilly fog shrouded the tower. She tried to get up but she could only move her arms, the lower part of her body was numbed. She sat rubbing her legs, trying to restore life to them; when she climbed out of the chest and tried to stand up, her legs gave way and she sat down on the floor. When finally she stood up again stiffly, she held out her hand to Jan, but he shook his head and cowered in his corner.

She went to the seaward arch and looked down. She could barely discern the roof of Mrs. Ool's houseboat; the fog made their world very small. She suddenly felt she could do it. She lowered herself gingerly out of the arch, down onto the rooftop, and, straddling it, prized loose a tile. It slithered down the slope with a clatter, then there was a silence, and then a splash. The splash made her afraid, but only for a moment. She prized loose a second tile, it came away more easily than the first; it clattered down, bounced and splashed. She had to lie down to get at the tile below. Once that had slithered, bounced and splashed, she could put her foot down on the first rung of the ladder.

It took a long time to get all the way down. Halfway down, her knees started shaking, but she stuck to it doggedly, although the splashes came ever nearer. When at last she stood on the roof of the houseboat, she felt so shaky that she had to sit down. Now she looked up the slope, it seemed incredible to her that she had dared to do it; but the thought of staying where she was and leaving the others to their fate did not occur to her. The fog became lighter and started to lift, then it closed in again. As it closed in once more, she felt safer, took a deep breath and climbed back to the belfry.

When she came back to it, it suddenly seemed much smaller. The open space between the arch and the chest that had seemed so endless when she had crawled across it the night before through the wind and the rain, carrying the hymnbooks, was only a few steps.

"Jan!" she said. "Come on, I've made a ladder!" Jan looked up at her from the chest, his blue eyes wide and frightened. He had not moved in the meantime. "I—I thought you'd gone away," he said. "Haven't you heard me calling? Where were you?"

"On Mrs. Ool's houseboat," she said. "I've thrown off the roof tiles and made a ladder. Come on. You take Bussy and I'll take Ko and Noisette. Let's go down, quick, before it gets frightening."

Jan looked at her, his chin trembling. "I thought you were dead," he said.

"Wait," she said. "I've got a better idea. We'll take the ropes of our boats and tie them together and then I'll make a loop in the end and when you go down, you can hold on to it, and then I'll pull it up again and put the loop round the animals one by one and lower them down to you. Come on!"

She detached a rope from the broomstick they had used for a mast, then she skipped to the other chest, forgetting Prince. As she stretched out her hand toward the rope, he jumped on to the edge and pecked at her. She jumped back with a cry, then she threw a hymnbook at him, shouting "Kscht! Go away! Go away, I tell you!" Prince jumped off the chest onto the floor and went for her, his neck outstretched, his wings spread. She darted aside and he forgot about her. He strutted pompously toward the arch, lifted his head to crow, made a noise like tearing paper, then he sneezed. It stunned him, and he stood tottering for a moment, shaking his comb; then he tried again, stretched his neck, made a swanlike movement and squeaked. During all this, Adinda had loosened the rope from the mast of his chest. When he turned round and saw her there, he flew at her once more and, as she darted away, he jumped back into his domain.

When Adinda had knotted the ropes together, she went to get Jan. At first, he didn't dare to come out, but she managed to coax him to the arch, holding his hand. As he looked down the slope, he said tearfully, "I don't want to. I'm afraid."

"Don't be silly," she said. "I did it twice. It's very easy. You just lower yourself onto the top of the roof and then you go down the little ladder sideways. All you've got to do is to take off your clogs."

"No," he said, "I don't want to. I want to wait for Father."

"We'll wait for him down there. Let me show you. I'll go first and you follow and, if you slip, I'll catch you. Watch!" She sat down in the arch, her legs dangling outside; then she rolled over on her stomach, said, "Watch!" again, and lowered herself onto the rooftop. He peeped down at her, his head very small in the arch of the tower. "Come on!" she called. "Do the same. Swing your legs out!" He obeyed. "Now roll over on your stomach!" "I daren't," he whimpered, "come back!"

Then she said it. She had thought of it all along, in case he wouldn't come. "If you don't," she called, "I'll go and leave you —with her!"

Jan stared at her in horror, then he began to cry.

"Roll over!" she shouted. "Do as you're told!"

He rolled over, crying.

"Now lower yourself down, quick, and spread your legs!"

He lowered himself, but he had no strength left, so his hands slipped and he fell, straddling the rooftop. For a moment, he sat motionless without uttering a sound, then he started to rock, bawling in anguish. She tried to comfort him by putting her arms around him, saying, "Don't! Don't! You're safe now." But he wouldn't stop. When in the end she got him so far that he started sidling down the ladder holding her hand, he was still bawling. He didn't stop until they had finally reached Mrs. Ool's roof, where he lay down, his head on his arms, crying.

She hesitated, then she scrambled back up the ladder, to the top of the roof, then up into the belfry. From the arch, Noisette was watching her. She took the rope and went to put the loop round Noisette's neck, but she didn't succeed. Noisette darted away playfully, and each time she stretched out her hand toward her, the kitten skipped aside at the very last moment. She decided to start with Ko.

He still sat in the chest, his ears flat, his eyes closed, busy breathing. She passed the rope round his chest behind his forelegs, and he let her fumble without so much as opening his eyes. Then she lifted him by the ears, carried him to the arch and called, "Jan! Watch out! Jan!" As he looked up, she started lowering Ko. Ko remained exactly as he was, his front paws begging, his hind legs dangling. She had to swing him, to make him slide down the right side of the roof; then he bumped passively from tile to tile until Jan, who had got stiffly to his feet, could catch him. Jan took him into his arms and loosened the rope; when he put him down, Ko started hopping and sniffing at once.

Bussy was more difficult. He had been watching, and when she came for him he ran away; but his hind legs ran faster than his front ones, so he stumbled; as he slithered on his chin she caught him. He started yelping as she picked him up, scrabbled in the air with his hind paws, but she managed to pass the loop round his chest and carried him quickly to the arch. As she lowered him, he hung spread-eagled, turning, and half-way down to the rooftop he started making water. She had to swing him too, to make him go down the right side; as soon as he hit the roof of the church he tried to hold on to it. Half-way down the ladder he succeeded. She called to Jan, "Call him!" and Jan called, "Bussy! Bussy! Here, boy!" but Bussy didn't budge, and crouched on the slope like a frog, whimper-ing. She had to throw three hymnbooks before he shied and lost his foothold. She let him slither very fast; when Jan finally caught him, took off the rope and put him down, he lay down and bawled as Jan had done.

Noisette refused to be caught, so there was nothing for it but to go down and hope that she would follow. When Adinda sat straddling the roof on her way down, the fog lifted. A gust of wind rolled away the mist that had shrouded the tower, and as she sat there, she saw the sea again down below, the distant roof-tops, the drowned trees. Suddenly, she was afraid; when Jan called her she closed her eyes, swallowed and started to descend the ladder trembling. The wind tugged at her skirt; halfway down, it caught on a nail. When the jerk came, she still had her eyes closed, and it was so unexpected that she nearly lost her balance. She stifled a cry and clung to the ladder, unable to move.

"Adinda!" Jan's voice called. "Adinda, come down!"

She shut her eyes again, and tears ran down her nose. She could no longer control her trembling, and she knew she couldn't move another step. As she lay there, with that panic slowly overpowering her once more, this time without meeting any resistance, there came, from quite close, a soft "miaow." She looked up, her mouth open, shaking, and saw Noisette just above her, upside down on the ladder, thrashing her tail. She swallowed once more and, without taking her eyes off Noisette, slowly lowered herself into the emptiness, her foot groping for the next step. There was a tearing noise as the nail ripped her skirt, then it got stuck on the hem. She fumbled for it with one hand, not daring to breathe. When she found it, she swallowed again, shut her eyes, and with a last desperate courage, tore it free. After that, she went limp, overcome by weakness. Noisette piloted her down.

When her right foot at last touched the houseboat, she didn't know what to do. Her other foot found nothing. Then she felt Jan's hands on her waist, gently pulling, and she slumped backward into his arms.

As the children climbed into Mrs. Ool's houseboat through the lavatory window, they entered a fairy world, one they had often vaguely dreamed of, just before falling asleep.

There it was: a tiny house, complete with all the familiar household objects, only much smaller, as if they were made to play with. Everything was small: the stove in the kitchen, the pots and pans, the kitchen table and its stools; then there was the bedroom, six foot by four, with a narrow bunk, a tiny washstand, a small wardrobe and, in front of the bed, a pair of floppy slippers with parrots embroidered upon them. They just fitted Adinda. Then there was the little hall with the canary, that looked faint and bedraggled. The first thing they did was to fill its tiny drinking cup with water from the kitchen and give it a teaspoonful of bird seed that Adinda had found on the shelf. It was the top shelf in the kitchen, but both of them could reach it easily. On it was a row of tins, painted blue, with labels saying, "Tea," "Coffee," "Sugar," "Sweet Lime" and "Bird Seed."

It was the sitting room that delighted them most. The smallest sitting room in the world, with a miniature open fireplace, two little tub chairs, a small round table, and, against the walls, on one side, a doll's tea set and a small couch with two cushions on it, one embroidered with the legend "Good Night," and the other with "Good Morning"; on the other side a desk and a miniature upright piano with a keyboard only a yard wide. As Jan opened the lid, he found on its keys a velvet runner with "God Is Music" embroidered upon it.

Jan sat down at once to play, and left it to Adinda to get the animals in. She fed them after she had found bread, sour milk and a sausage in the kitchen cupboard and, underneath the sink, two enamel dishes, one red and the other blue, the first saying, "Fido," and the second "Kitty." She looked for one marked "Bunny," but as she couldn't find it, she gave Ko a small enamel wash basin marked "Happy Feet." As the animals were eating, and Jan plonking "Chopsticks" on the piano, Adinda went into the bedroom, opened the wardrobe and looked at the clothes. Her own were wet and torn, so she took them off and put on a set of pink woolen underwear, a black skirt that was much too wide, a lacy blouse with a ruffle round the neck and a black knitted cardigan with glass eyes for buttons, which also was much too wide. As she looked at herself in the mirror on the inside of the wardrobe door, she looked exactly like Mrs. Ool. The cardigan was a little disturbing for the glass eyes squinted in all directions, but she felt grown up and dignified. She also found a black bonnet that covered just the back of the head and tied under the chin with velvet ribbons. There were two little slits in the sides, through which she first pulled her plaits and then her ears. She looked at herself all the time, getting more and more satisfied with the result. She opened a drawer and found a necklace of black glass beads with a medallion attached to it, showing the portrait of a man with a mustache, resting his chin on a finger. She put it on. There were also a number of rings, but they were too big, and a fan which, when opened, showed the picture of a kitten in a boot. She hesitated between the fan and Mrs. Ool's trumpet, which hung beside the bed. She blew the trumpet, but it wouldn't make a sound, so she decided on the fan. There were earrings too, two pairs of them, one made of black jet, the other amber. She tried to pierce an ear, but it hurt, so she regretfully put them back in the drawer. Then she found a watch on a silver chain. She put it round her neck. The watch and the medallion clinked together as she walked, so she pinned them down with a glass brooch saying "Mother," embellished with pink rosebuds. Then she went to the kitchen and drank three glasses of water.

Jan was playing, "Can You Wash Your Father's Shirt." Noisette was sniffing gingerly round the kitchen, Bussy was lapping clean all the plates, and Ko had hiccoughs, sitting in the middle of the floor, his eyes closed. One of the kitchen windows was broken and the curtains fluttered out of it. She climbed onto a stool and pulled them in, taking care not to cut herself. She saw that there were shutters outside, so she opened the window cautiously and closed them. Then she lit the stove.

Half an hour later they were eating. She had found everything in the kitchen cupboard, and laid the table. When she went to call Jan as the eggs were done, he didn't want to come at first, saying he was the captain. Then, seeing her clothes and her jewels, he became jealous and wanted to dress up too. But by using the same words in the same voice as Mrs. Grijpma had, she managed to get him to the kitchen, made him wash his hands and comb his hair. When she told him to say Grace, he refused. He only did it when she told him that captains always said Grace. So he said Grace in a captain's voice; then he raised his glass of water and said, "Gentlemen, the Queen" and drank.

When they had finished eating, he refused to help with the washing up, and went to change. He came out in a flowered apron with a stocking tied round his middle, a red handkerchief round his neck, galoshes, and a black toque with osprey feathers round the crown. He rummaged in the desk in the sitting room, found an exercise book marked "Grocer" of which only four pages were used. He tore them out, found a pencil and started writing a book, called "A Naval Hero of 10 Years Old." He wrote the "o" of "10" faintly, so that after his birthday he could change it into a "1." The first line was, "Once upon a time there was a boy called Jan who amazed all the persons with his currage"; then he started to play the piano again.

During the few hours after the meal, before the wind started to blow again, Adinda was so happy that it made her sad. The mixture of her races and the things that had happened to her had made her incapable of sustained enjoyment. Whenever she got a toy that delighted her, she became sad; for from the moment she first set eyes on it, something inside her only waited for it to be broken. On board Mrs. Ool's houseboat, that wonderful doll's house in fairyland, she sat, dressed up and sad, on the couch with the two cushions, her legs folded under her, her hands in her lap, waiting.

Jan knew those moods of hers by experience. They always ended by maddening him with a feeling of unfairness. There she would sit, all the tools of happiness around her, and she would refuse to play, just sit and gaze at something that seemed to happen not outside, but within her. Whenever he asked, "What's the matter?" she would answer, "Nothing," in a quiet voice that was almost condescending, as if he could not be expected to understand. She would overcast the sky and take away the luster of even the most wonderful toys by just sitting, her hands in her lap, staring at nothing.

This afternoon it was the same. She refused to play, just sat there and stared; when asked what was the matter, she answered, "Nothing," and after Jan had tried in vain to defend his joy against the gathering darkness of her unfair and maddening gloom, he ended as always in a somber and destructive mood. Had he been older, he would have hit her; he kicked the desk, hammered brutally on the piano, slammed the lid shut with such violence that the wires hummed and ended up on his back in front of the fireplace, holding Noisette back by her tail until she growled, lashed out and scratched him, and he flung her in a corner. Then he started pestering Ko by sticking a poker under his behind whenever he sat down to snooze.

Adinda sat watching him without expression, darkly comforted by the triumph of her sadness. As Noisette growled and Ko scurried away and Jan lay loutishly on the floor, deliberately belching, she shut her eyes and listened to the wind rising and the toneless lapping of the waves, feeling like crying but incapable of tears, accepting as inevitable the misery she had brought about herself by imposing on her world the gloom life had taught her to expect.

As the wind rose, the waves became bigger and the little houseboat started to rock. Jan was the first to feel the sickness rise inside him, and he went to the lavatory to vomit after he had lain thinking about it for a long time. As he opened the lavatory door, a gust of wind blew through the open window and from behind the lavatory basin a demon sprang, screeching and flapping. It was Prince. He stormed into the sitting room, his short wings spread, his neck outstretched, causing havoc and panic as he ran; Jan fled into the bedroom, screaming, Prince at his heels; then Jan jumped out again, slamming the door behind him. Inside the evil bird could be heard scratching, crowing hoarsely, muttering in the dusk.

As Jan came back to the sitting room, he was crying. He slumped on the couch, his head on his arms, and when Adinda stretched out a slim hand toward him, he kicked her. She got up, her jewels clinking, teetered to the lavatory, holding onto the chairs, the piano and the doorpost, and was sick without a sound.

When she came back to the couch, she curled up beside Jan's prostrate body and, one by one, the animals joined them, as darkness fell. The little boat pitched and rocked, its bow creaked in the hole of the roof, the waves thumped against its stern, and the showers of spray streaked the roof like squalls of rain. After darkness, the wind brought occasionally, between two showers, a distant wailing, high bodiless cries for help, that had not been heard before. The children heard it in their sleep, and stirred uneasily; without their knowing it, the ebbing tide had detached the houseboat from the roof and carried it off, past the sunken trees and the broken roofs, seaward.

When they woke up, the tide had changed, the wind had started to blow again and the little houseboat was drifting inland once more. As they looked through the windows they saw nothing but water. The village had gone, so had the church. They seemed to drift in an empty world of gray choppy waves, underneath a tremendous sky full of slowly sailing clouds, reddened by the rising sun. The boat drifted sideways, rolling. The pans clanked in the kitchen with a slow rhythmic clatter; the iron basket in the fireplace slid to and fro with a grating sound; the swinging oil lamp squeaked at the ceiling. They drifted through this gray emptiness for some time, without it getting lighter. The sun rose behind the rolling clouds, sending vague fields of darkness sliding across the gray plain, and the children thought they were at sea until they saw a small speck in the distance, slowly drawing nearer.

At first they thought it was a buoy: a dark oblong object with a silver spire. As they drifted nearer, they saw it was a horse, its head and haunches just out of the water, standing motionlessly in the waves with a heron on its back. They came so close that they could see the horse was asleep. It had its eyes closed, and at every wave it slowly lifted its head, to let it slowly sink back again. When they were very near, the heron spread its wings and rose, its long legs dangling; then it swerved over the water, its neck arched, its legs stretched out behind it, rose without moving its wings in a long sweep to the sky, and sailed out of sight. The horse never opened its eyes, although they tapped on the window and called "Horsey, horsey! Tuk, tuk!" as they had heard Farmer Bouma do.

After the horse, other small objects slowly drew nearer from the sea, as they bobbed inland sideways, rocking. A telegraph pole, heeling over, its wires trailing like hanging hair, moving with the current; a swaying tree, looking as if it were sailing; then a small orchard with, suspended in the branches, a big black rubber dinghy. At a hundred yards' distance was a corner of a ruin that had been a house, a right angle of jagged walls, and over it peered the mad motionless face of a man. The man frightened them as he drew inexorably nearer, the corner of his house cleaving the waves like the bow of a ship. He stared at them with dark, menacing eyes, his hair moving in the wind; then, suddenly he climbed over the wall and jumped into the water. He swam toward them with wild dog-like strokes, and they stared at him, horrified, unable to look away. But luckily he vanished in the water before he could grab their boat; when they looked back they saw with relief that there was nothing but the ruin, the orchard, the distant dinghy and the waves.

As they drifted on, the low black pyramids of farmhouse roofs glided past them. All of them had white flags fluttering out of the attic windows, and occasionally heads looked at them and shouted; but no one jumped at them any more. Toward noon, there was a low droning sound and as they peered out they saw a huge dragonfly approaching, skimming the waves. It was a blue airplane, a single man inside, wearing goggles, who waved at them as he swooped round, and they waved back. They ran to the other window and saw the plane fly away, low on the water toward the roofs they had passed. It circled round them, its blue wings glinting as it tilted, and flew on until it vanished in the distance, a speck in the sky. They drifted past a village with lots of people on the rooftops who waved and called. They waved back and, as Bussy yapped excitedly, Jan lifted him in his arms to let him see. On the outskirts of the village was a big farm, with a whole family on its roof, a father, a mother and four children. They all had cushions strapped to their backs, and when the houseboat drifted slowly past, they waved and called too.

After that, there came a long stretch of nothing. Not a pole, not a tree, just the waves and a faint green haze on the horizon. Adinda cut some bread and buttered it and took it to Jan, because he didn't want to come to the kitchen. She couldn't get him away from the window; he ate his bread without knowing what he was doing, leaning with his elbows on the window sill. She fed the animals and, as there was nothing to see but the water and the sky, she lay down on the couch and tried to sleep. But every time she dozed off, the ship rolled and she had to clutch the edge of the couch so as not to fall off. In the end, she got up again and joined Jan at the window to stare at the sea, and at the distant green haze from which now the ghost of a church tower was emerging. Then there was another droning noise that hovered around them, high up in the sky. After they had run from one window to the other, peering up at the clouds to see what it was, it finally came into view; a black machine like a June bug, a huge round wing thrashing above it. They had never seen a helicopter before, and as it slowly lowered itself, roaring, they saw, inside the glass cupola in front, a big Negro with a bright yellow cap on stare at them, and then wave. They waved back hesitantly; the Negro's grin flashed white in his round black face. He hung staring and grinning at them for a long while, his machine bobbing up and down in the wind with a roar that made the windows rattle; then he scratched his head, and rose straight up into the sky, the roar of his machine diminishing until it was gone.

They saw more helicopters as they approached the shore toward nightfall. They saw, in the distance, the strange June bugs hover over rooftops, slowly descend with a rope hanging out of their stomachs and rise up again with a cluster of people clinging to it. They carried the people slowly through the air to the crown of the dike, where they gingerly put them down again.

There wasn't a boat in sight. It seemed as if everything that once had been afloat on the waters of Holland had been washed away. They saw their first boat toward nightfall, after they had run aground near a gap in the dike. The houseboat had bumped a few times, then it had settled, slightly on one side. While the waves slowly drew back, until they were just a slight ripple above a sandy shoal, there came from the narrowing darkness the slow chug-chug of an engine, and they saw loom up behind them a strange gray vessel, loaded with oblong boxes, stacked on its deck. As the vessel drew near a head with a sailor's cap was silhouetted against the dark red sky as it peered at them over the boxes, its ribbons flying. It was a Navy launch, loaded with coffins, and when it was only a few yards distant, it ran aground. The engine chugged and churned, yellow foam floated toward them as the propeller stirred the mud: then it stopped and fell silent. They were alone in the great swishing darkness of the waves and the sky, with this strange angular vessel dumbly staring at them.

Some time later, when only a red seam of the day still lingered far away in the sky, a light shone on them, playing over the windows, and they heard sloshing steps draw near. Someone tapped on the window and Adinda lit the lamp, although Jan, cowering in a corner, whispered, "Don't! Don't!" In the lamplight, they saw a face peer at them between two hands, and they heard a voice call, faintly, "Open up!" Adinda opened the window and they saw a sailor, his cap on his eyebrows, the strap around his chin, looking like a monk in his hooded duffel coat. "What are you doing here?" the sailor asked, sternly.

Adinda answered, "Playing."

"Is this your ship?"

Adinda shook her head.

"Where are your parents?"

Adinda said, "Dead."

The sailor looked at her, his blue eyes narrowed. "Are they in here?" he asked.

Adinda shook her head once more. "They were buried underneath the waringin," she said. "I don't know where his are. Mrs. Grijpma is lying in the tower, and Mr. Grijpma didn't come back. I don't know what happened to Mrs. Ool."

The sailor nodded thoughtfully and said, "I see." Then he looked round the little room and saw the animals.

"Are they yours?" he asked.

Adinda nodded. "We saved them," she said. "They were in the belfry."

"Where?" the sailor asked, turning one ear toward her, frowning.

"In the belfry," she said. "That's where we went to ring the bells."

The sailor nodded, looking at her thoughtfully. "Where are you from?" he asked, at last.

"We're from Niewerland," Adinda answered.

"What is your name?"

"Adinda de la Maison Rouge."

The sailor looked at her as if he were getting angry. "And who is he?" he asked, nodding at Jan.

Adinda's lip began to tremble, but she answered bravely, "Jan Brink."

The sailor said, "Mm," then he rubbed his chin. He hadn't shaved for a long time, and he looked very tired. "How does one get into this thing?"

"Through the front door," she said. "It's on the other side."

He vanished from the window and his sucking steps went slowly round the boat. "Don't open," Jan whispered, as he saw Adinda go toward the door, "Don't let him in! Shut the window!" But Adinda ignored him. She went to the hall, opened the door and let the sailor in. He climbed onto the threshold, sat down and took his boots off, which he put on the floor inside. Ko came hopping toward them, sniffed and crawled inside one. The sailor didn't notice. He was very big; when he stood up he hit his head. He took off his cap, his hair was flat and very blond. He looked less alarming without his cap.

"Well," he said, looking round the hall. "It seems we're to be neighbors for some hours." Then he scratched the bars of the canary's cage, said, "Tweet, tweet," and as the canary said nothing, he asked, "Does he sing?"

"Oh yes," said Adinda, "but I don't think he will now. I think he's been seasick. We were seasick too, and when Jan opened the lavatory door, Prince came out. He must have slid down the roof all by himself, without our seeing him. Jan locked him in the bedroom."

"Is that where he is now?" the sailor asked, frowning.

Adinda nodded.

"Where is it?"

She pointed at the bedroom door; when he went toward it she said pleadingly, "Please don't! If you let him out, we'll never get him in again, and he'll break everything. Please don't."

The sailor said, soothingly, "Ssh, ssh," and opened the bedroom door. Adinda flattened herself against the wall and bit her knuckles. The sailor peered cautiously into the dark bedroom; then he opened the door wider and was about to step inside, when Prince dashed out between his legs, screeching, and stormed toward the sitting room. The sailor jumped, hit his head again and cursed; then he went into the sitting room and tried to catch Prince, making clucking noises. Prince ran round the sitting room twice, shrieking; then he stormed back into the

[61]

bedroom and Adinda pulled the door shut. The sailor sat down gingerly on the couch, wiped his forehead with the back of his hand and said, "Now you come and sit down beside me, and let's get this straight." He looked at Jan, who still sat cowering in the corner; he took in the flowered apron, the galoshes, the toque with the osprey feathers; then he looked at Adinda again, stretched out his hand toward the medallion, looked at the man with the mustache, opened her fan and stared at the kitten in the boot. His eyes slowly traveled up the row of squinting buttons to the ruffle round her neck, the bonnet with the plaits and the ears sticking out. "Where did you find these clothes?" he asked.

"In the wardrobe in the bedroom," Adinda answered.

"Whose are they?"

"Mrs. Ool's."

"And who is Mrs. Ool?"

"The old woman who lived here."

"Where is she now?"

Adinda shrugged her shoulders. Jan said, "She was taken out during Jake's funeral by a fat man who pulled her through the window. She was in her underskirt."

The sailor said, "Mm," and nodded, then he said, "So your parents are—gone."

The children nodded.

The sailor looked at them and they saw, to their amazement and alarm, his weary eyes fill with tears. "Jesus," he said, "this is a God-awful mess."

The blasphemy did not upset them. It only made them realize that he was filled with kindness toward them, and that he was very tired.

"Well," he said, "don't you worry. There are thousands of

dead, you're not the only ones. You're safe now. Whatever this flood has done, it has turned us all into one family." Then he got up, opened the window and shouted, "Boys, put out the anchor and come over here! And bring some food, there are children here!" A voice answered from the darkness; then many sucking steps drew near. Faces with caps peered through the window, and they came in, four of them, all with big muddy boots on, which they took off at the door. They were unshaven and dirty and one of them, who had red hair and freckles, carried an armful of shiny new tins. "Well, well," he said, "who's granny?" Adinda said, "I'm Adinda de la Maison Rouge," and the freckled sailor whistled. "Where's the stove, bos'n?" he asked, and their new friend answered, "There's a galley along the corridor there. But take it easy, it's like a doll's house. This boat must have been built for a midget."

The other sailors looked round the sitting room in wonder. They took off their caps, and one of them started to sit down in one of the tub chairs, but the bos'n cried "Hey!" and so he sat down on the floor. A thin one with a big head and a face like a friendly dog took out a mouth organ, said, "Listen to this," and started to play "Little Cart down Sandy Road." "Know that one?" he asked Jan, after the first bars.

"Yes," said Jan. "I can sing it."

"Good," said the sailor. "Let's have it." He started again, and Jan sang it, but with difficulty, for it was pitched very high. When they had finished, the sailor asked, "What else do you know? 'The Windmill Song?'"

"No," said Jan. "I know 'All Ye Prisoners Arise.'"

The sailors laughed, and the man with the mouth organ said, "That's a good one. Let's go. But don't squeak: sing. Is this better?" and he blew a chord.

[63]

Jan nodded and sang. The sailors sat on the floor, looking at his apron and his toque, their faces blank. The bos'n in the corner covered his face with his hands; when Jan had sung two more songs, and the freckled one came in with the food, the bos'n shook his head when he was offered the plate marked "Kitty."

The children felt safe now, and Jan became overexcited. He wanted the animals to do tricks for the sailors, and when he didn't succeed, he started to sing again. His thin voice trilled and warbled, his eyes shone and his ears were bright red.

Adinda sat on the couch, her legs folded, her hands in her lap, watching the weeping man.

What seemed something special and rare at first, something that was part of a dream, proved to be reality. With the tidal wave, a wave of kindness had swept the country, washing everything before it.

Until the night the sailors came, the children had lived warily in an indifferent and often hostile world of grownups, who tolerated them only as long as they watched out for the first signs of irritation, which they had soon come to recognize. Now, all of a sudden, the grownups surrounding them had changed. They were dazed and stunned, as if after a fall, noticed the children for the first time and took them to their hearts with a warmth that was almost overwhelming.

At the end of that night of the mouth organ, the children finally dropped with fatigue. The sailors put them to bed on the couch, and in their half-sleep they heard them softly talking; the bos'n said, "Ssh!" every time they stirred. They fell asleep in the spicy smell of pipe tobacco and, during the night, when occasionally they awoke feeling lost, there was always someone sitting near them, watching them. Jan was carried asleep to the lavatory by the dog-faced sailor, who gingerly took down his trousers and put him on the seat, and when Jan mumbled, "Play," he softly played his mouth organ in his cupped hands. When Adinda woke up toward sunrise, the freckled sailor put his hand on her forehead and said, "Don't worry. I'm here. Count sheep," and she fell asleep again thinking of his hand, which smelled of bully beef.

The next morning, they were woken up with steaming mugs of tea and biscuits with sugar and butter and a present for Jan: a beautiful penknife. The wind had risen once more, the boat was rocking, and the bos'n explained to them that they shouldn't be afraid now, they were going to be towed inland to a little village called Onderkerk. The village was all broken and there were no people there except soldiers and sailors but, from there, they would be sent to very kind people on the dry land where they would have lots of toys and lovely beds to sleep in and as much food as they liked, and they would soon forget it all.

The children listened to him earnestly, and did not dare to show their disappointment when he said that they were to forget it all. Jan was sure that if he could manage to wring out some tears in an hour or so, the dog-faced sailor would give him his mouth organ, and Adinda was thinking hard about a means of keeping her jewels and the fan.

The bos'n and three of the sailors put on their high boots to wade back to their launch. As the bos'n pulled on his left boot, he jumped and cursed and hopped backward on one foot until he hit the wall. He turned the boot upside down, and Ko fell out.

[66]

The freckled one stayed with them. There was a lot of shouting, ropes splashed in the water and thumped on the roof, and while the freckled one stood shouting, "Easy! Easy!" out of the window, the boat moved. The children stood looking out of the window at a fishing smack coming out of a hole in the dike. The fishing smack looked primitive and rusty, and on its buckled bow two letters and a number were painted: *UK 516*.

"That's a fisherman from Urk," the freckled sailor said. "The number of people those pirates have saved, you wouldn't believe it. They sail right inland with those damn boats of theirs, right into the villages and up the streets. Pity they won't co-operate."

Then there was a sudden jerk, a twang of snapping wire, and the freckled sailor fell on his back. As he jumped up again, thoroughly rattled, he tore open the window and shouted. The houseboat turned until it was lying cross-seas again, rolling madly, and then, just as the children began to be afraid, a huge rusty wall slid past the window with a scraping noise, and the freckled sailor ran to the front door. There was a lot of shouting again, and then he came running back, while the houseboat bumped against the gray wall with splintering crashes. He called, "Come on children! Out you go!" Adinda cried, "The animals! The animals!" and the sailor said nervously, "All right, all right, get them!" Adinda grabbed Ko and Noisette, Jan took Bussy in his arms. Adinda was lifted out first. "I'm going to put you onto the roof," the sailor said. "Run for the ship. They'll lift you on board. Up you go." She vanished from sight, and Jan heard her steps run across the roof. Then it was his turn, and both Bussy and he were very much afraid. Bussy wriggled and yelped, Jan whimpered. The sailor patted him on the back, picked him up and pushed him up onto the roof. The houseboat was rocking so much that when Jan tried to run he staggered back several times; over the rail of the fishing smack, a row of grim pirates stood looking at him, swarthy heads with very blue eyes, wearing fur caps and earrings. When finally he tottered close enough, one of the pirates put out two huge hands, grabbed him by the shoulders of his apron and swung him on board like a cat. As his galoshes thumped on the iron deck, Jan's knees gave way, and then one of the pirates, a giant in short baggy trousers, wrinkled black stockings and the biggest clogs he had ever seen, stooped and picked him up. He breathed a smell like petrol in Jan's face as his deep voice said, "That's my little man! How are you, Noah?"; then he kissed him with cheeks like rasps. When Jan was put down again, he saw that Adinda was being fondled by a short, square one, who wore a wide-brimmed bowler hat; the square one took hold of his hand too, without putting Adinda down, and said, "You come with me. Yum, yum. Big boy." As he was being towed along, Jan saw the launch with the coffins bob up and down close by, and he heard the huge pirate who had kissed him shout between his hands, "We'll hand them over to the hospital ship! Pick up that houseboat! Learn how to sail!" Then he came clumping after them. A bell rang somewhere in the depths, the ship trembled as an engine started chugging and a thin pipe between the masts started blowing black rings, that were whisked off by the wind.

They were taken to a small, dark galley, with a stove full of hissing pans. The square pirate put Adinda down on a narrow bench in front of the stove; then he picked up Jan and put him down beside her. He took two mugs from a row that dangled rocking from the ceiling, and then the galley became pitch dark as the huge captain blotted out the doorway. "Well, well," his deep voice grumbled, "and where are you from, people?"

Adinda said, in a small voice, "Niewerland, sir."

The pirate grunted. "Ah," he said, "now you're on the island of Urk. Do you know that it is the biggest island in the Zuider Zee, if you count the decks of its ships?"

Adinda swallowed and said, "Yes, sir."

"Ah," said the pirate, "where would Holland be without the island of Urk? You'd all drown like rats if we left you to the Navy. Welcome to Urk, people. Give me a kiss, little Negro. I'm your uncle, the captain." He stooped down and there was a sound as if a boot were pulled out of the mud. Then his deep voice said to the square one, "Give them to eat, Urker. Take my sugar, and when you've finished with them, hand them down to the fo'c'sle. We'll dress them like Christians and put them to bed. This rabbit yours?

Adinda nodded, speechless.

"Ah," said the captain, "that's nice of you. Stew tonight, Urker. We're all sick of your slimy fish."

Adinda, in a high, strained voice, said quaveringly, "He's not for eating! He can think."

"Ah," said the captain, "if thinking could keep you out of the pot, a lot more people would be high and dry just now."

Adinda tried to speak, but she couldn't. Jan said hastily, "If you'd like some nice stew, sir, there's a lovely fat cock on board the houseboat. Ko is very thin really, all fur and buttons."

The huge pirate said, "Ah," again, with another smell of petrol; then he grunted, "If he's a friend of yours, we'll feed him too, dress him like a Christian and put him to bed. Do you hear me, Urker? One more plate for the rabbit tonight, and keep your hands behind your back."

The square one said, "What about giving this stove some air? You're blocking the draft. And stop frightening those kids. Look for someone your own size."

"Ah," said the captain, getting up. "D'you hear that, people?

That's the way ships from the island of Urk are sailed. No megaphones, no whistles like in the Navy. Listen to this Urker, giving his skipper the big mouth. That's what it says in the Bible: all ye men be brethren. This is freedom, people, and that goes for you too, little daughter of Ham." There was another sound of a boot being pulled out of the mud, and the dark shape wheeled away. Adinda sat blinking in the sunlight, rubbing her cheek, her lip trembling. "Here, kiddies," the square one said, holding out two steaming mugs. "Drink that, and don't mind the skipper. He doesn't mean any harm. Tonight he'll be playing marbles with you. How many other people are there? Didn't I see a cat?"

Jan nodded. "And there's Bussy," he said. "Bussy, Bussy, Bussy!"

There was a sound of scrabbling paws on the iron deck outside, and Bussy peeped over the high threshold, his floppy ears pricked up. "Ah," said the square one. "Is that him?" He stooped and shook Bussy's front paw. "Happy to know you, Bussy," he said. "I'm the cook. Do you like fish?" Bussy started licking his hand. "I see you do. Come in," and he lifted him inside by the scruff of his neck. Out of the belly of the stove he took a very dirty dish with bits of fish in it, and put it down for Bussy. "Don't burn your nose, Bussy," he said. "Sailors' food is piping hot." Then Noisette's small head peeked in, in the bottom left-hand corner, her nose level with the threshold. "Ah," said the cook. "And who might this be?"

"Noisette," Jan answered.

"Come in, Noisette. Take your time. All friendly people here. But don't hurry if you don't feel like it. You're in a free country now."

Noisette considered the plate of fish, and as the cook turned

[70]

away from her, she stretched her neck and showed the whole of her head. Then something clattered on the stove and she ducked.

"Noisette," Jan called. "Pst! Pst!"

Her head appeared again, and she made a great show of sniffing at the threshold. Jan stretched out his hand toward her, but she darted off.

"Never hurry a woman, boy," the cook said. "It's more blessed to give than to receive. The sooner you learn that, the happier you'll be. Isn't that so, young woman?"

Adinda looked at him warily with her almond-shaped eyes.

The cook poked his nose, then he said, wiping his finger on the seat of his trousers, "That's right. Rule the world with your black jets and your moonstones. Ah, the sweet joy of suffering. Drink your tea while it's hot."

Adinda didn't move.

The cook sighed. "That's right: don't drink your tea while it's hot. Punish us by refusing what you're dying to do. Come in, cat."

Noisette stared at him, from the right hand corner of the doorway now, with the same wary look that Adinda had given him.

The cook nodded. "That's right," he said. "Every day I wake up thankful that God didn't make me beautiful. We drink our tea while it's hot, don't we, boy? We look at the black hair spread out on the pillow and say, 'I love you,' instead of peeking up and saying, 'Do you know the ceiling needs a coat of whitewash?' " He raised his mug, said, "Bless you, boy. Here's to freedom and innocence," and drank with the sound of an emptying bath. Jan drank too, feeling manly and proud, and burned his lips. Adinda glanced at him as he winced.

Then Noisette slipped in and rubbed her arched back against

Adinda's leg. "Go on," said the cook, "pretend. We believe you. Ah, the softness of a woman's lie." Then he drank some more of his tea, slobbering.

Jan looked at him with a grown-up face and said, "I want to be cremated," the most adult thing he could think of. The cook looked at him broodingly through the steam of his cup, then he said, "Well, boy, after that, who can say there is no God?"

"Fons," said Jan. "He said to Papa Donker 'Listen.' And then he took out his watch and then he said, 'God, if You exist, strike me dead within two minutes' and then he went on digging and Papa Donker stood looking at him and said, 'God's minutes are bigger than yours.' "

"Good for him," said the cook. "What were they digging?"

"A grave," Jan answered, "for Henny Pronk's mother."

The cook shook his head and said, "Lucky woman. That's the secret of their self-confidence, if you ask me. They are always sure to get a grave. Well . . ." he took another sip of his tea, "this flood ought to shake them." Then he shrugged his shoulders. "But considering the other ones didn't," he continued, "let's ditch this foolish hope," and he threw the rest of his tea out of the door.

Jan heaved a happy sigh. All his life he had dreamed of talking man's talk, and suddenly here, on board this rusty ship, from the mouth of a real pirate wearing earrings, a necklace and a bowler hat, came the kind of words his mind had always vainly groped for. Just words, full of strength, wisdom and music, that meant nothing but freedom. "I've started a book called 'A Naval Hero of Ten Years Old,' " he said. "I left it in the houseboat. I hope Prince won't eat it."

"The Prince of Darkness," said the cook, taking a swig from a bottle, "eats the future. Look at the apple."

Jan asked, "Where?"

The cook took his mouth from the bottle and gazed at him, amazed. "What do you mean—where? There needn't be an apple, for a man to see one. Think of the apple: ripe and shiny in the trembling foliage of the tree. What's in its heart?"

"Pips," Jan answered.

"Apart from that," said the cook. "What else? We were talking about the Prince of Darkness, eating the future."

"I don't know," Jan said, disappointedly.

Adinda said, "Worms."

"Ah," said the cook, pointing at her with the bottle. "Trust a woman." Then he looked at Noisette, wolfing fish. "There you are," he said. "Now, just tell me, what was all the song and dance for? I knew that she was dying to eat that fish, we all knew it and, by God, she has managed to make us feel grateful. That's what we are, my boy: man, forever bewildered by the mystery of his rib."

Heavy steps came ringing along the deck, and an old man with a hairy nose and tufts growing out of his ears poked his head into the galley. "Come out, Urker," he said. "We're sailing inland, man the pole."

"Coming, Urker," Cook said. "You didn't bring your mug back."

"With my mug," the old man said, "I'll do as I damn well please."

When the old man was gone, Cook stood staring at where he had been, shaking his head. "Freedom," he said. "Well, come on, I'll take you to the wheelhouse. You shall tell your children's children how the fat farmers of Holland were saved by the Christians from Urk."

He took them by the hand and towed them along the windy

deck to the steps of the wheelhouse on the ship's poop; Bussy followed them. He knocked on the door with his fist and as it was opened by the giant captain, he said, "No time to dress them, Urker. Stick 'em up here."

"All right," the captain said, holding out his enormous hand. "Climb in, little darkness." Adinda gathered up her skirts and the cook lifted her inside; then he took Jan under the arms and lifted him too, and then he put in Bussy. The captain pulled the wheelhouse door shut and pointed at a narrow bench against the back wall. "Sit down there, people," he said, "watch out sharply, and if you see anyone waving from the water, sing out."

The children sat close together on the little bench, shaking with the vibration of the engine. The wheelhouse rattled, clanked and clattered about them. There was a thick smell of oil and old grease, and the pipe the captain was smoking didn't smell as nice as the sailors' tobacco had the night before. It smelled like steaming wet hay. They looked out and saw that the ship was approaching a gap in the dike, beyond which an endless plain of water could be seen, dotted with trees and rooftops. They hoped the ship would stop rocking once they were inside.

Overhead a loud droning noise approached, and four airplanes raced into view, flying very low against the leaden sky. "Look at them!" the captain shouted over the pandemonium of his wheelhouse. "Thousands of them in the air, throwing rubber bathtubs, and all they do is drown people!" As he got no answer, he turned round. "It's true," he shouted. "They throw out those bloated things, the wind blows them away, people jump off their roofs to catch them, and drown. Let them throw baths at home, and leave this work to us. The whole of

Urk is here, people, three hundred ships. We haven't slept for four days and nights, and we won't sleep until the last living soul is picked out of the trees. All we ask of the Navy is to leave us alone. The Navy!" He spat, and shook brown drops out of the stem of his pipe, which added an acrid smell to the stench in the wheelhouse. "When we get to Bruinisse, you'll see them. Their whole fleet is there, guns, searchlights, airplanes, floating automobiles and all. But you won't see them in here. Those people can't fight a war unless there is an enemy." Then he started to sing, beating time on the wheel, "Hell, Damnation, Fire and Flood, Cannot crush the friend of God," ending with two blasts on the ship's siren.

As the ship approached a dotted line of partly submerged poplars, the captain pulled a handle, the bell rang in the depths and the engine slowed. As the ship was losing speed, a gray shadow crept alongside from behind them, another rusty bow with painted on it, "UK 320." On its foredeck stood two men with astrakhan caps, looking like hunchbacks as the wind filled their doublets. They were sounding the depth of the water with poles. "There goes Meter," the captain shouted. "The second-best sailor in the fleet." Then he filled his pipe, and continued, shouting, "His ship has a smaller draught than we have, so he creeps ahead to feel the way. Lot of bridges on this road."

The children saw no road, but as the ships started to follow the line of the treetops, hugging them closely, they saw on the other side the tips of telegraph poles, occasionally bared by the waves. At the end of the long line of trees was the silhouette of a village. "We hit a lorry here yesterday!" the captain shouted. "Meter had to push it right off the road. At least, we think it was a lorry because a spare wheel came floating up. It may have been a farmer's cart on rubber tires, but it didn't sound like it.

Now watch out. Here comes a bridge. There isn't as much swell as last night, but we may still scrape it." He stood waiting for something, his hand in the air, his mouth open. There was a bump and a scraping noise. "There you are," he said. "Now the road is clear until we get to that village over there, called Smorenburg. Ever been to Smorenburg, people?" The children shook their heads. "Nice place," the captain shouted. "I'd like to see its lower half some day. We picked that one clean yesterday. Now we're for the big farms beyond. Lots of people there, if the Navy hasn't drowned them." Then he fell silent, and the children began to feel sick. The ship rolled and clattered. The slow throb of the engine made them bounce on their bench. The captain hummed. Occasionally submerged branches scraped the hull, and once or twice there came a shout from out front, "Easy!" at which the captain shrugged his shoulders and interrupted his humming to say, "Pooh."

When they reached the first houses of the village, the captain lowered the windows of the wheelhouse by their leather straps and let the wind in. The explosions of the exhaust of the *UK 320* echoed like shots against the gables. The children forgot their sickness and peered out as the ship, slowly rolling, sailed up a narrow street of low houses. Between the rooftops beds were floating, and wreckage. When they passed a side street, they saw it was blocked by a big mossy thatched roof with a dead cat on it; the wind had filled the gap between the two rows of houses behind it with straw, onions, dead cattle and mattresses. From shattered windows curtains were blowing, and here and there white flags fluttered from the rooftops. "I wish everybody would do as we do," the captain said, "and take down those flags when the people are off." Then someone shouted from the foredeck, "Cut the engine! We're hailing." The captain pulled the handle, the bell rang and the engine fell silent. "Hurry up!" he shouted. "There's a lot of side wind!" The cook climbed onto the flat roof of his galley and shouted over the silent devastation. "Hallo! Anybody there? Hallo! Anybody there? Hallo . . . !" His voice echoed among the empty houses as he shouted in four directions, but there came no answer, only the swish of the waves and the banging of a shutter. "I'm pushing on, Urker!" the captain shouted, "before we get stuck on a roof!"

The bell rang again, the engine throbbed and the ship trembled as it gathered speed and slowly glided on along the street. They passed higher houses now, of which the top floors emerged from the water. Through the broken windows the children could see rooms with tables, and pictures on the walls, and beds. In one of them there were two small beds, and on a table just in front of the window stood a pair of woman's shoes, a cheese and a red toy fire engine. Jan cried, "Look! Urker, look! A fire engine!" but the captain was not listening. He stood staring intently ahead, his legs spread, both hands on the wheel. Jan gazed back at the fire engine until it vanished from sight.

They were entering a wide pond now, with choppy waves, which might be the village square. They were heading straight across it when suddenly the ship ahead gave three blasts on its siren. The captain's hand sprang at the handle, pulled it back, the bell rang and the engine stopped. Again, there was that hollow silence, with only the swishing of the waves and the low moaning of the wind in the rigging. A man on the back of the other ship shouted, between his hands, "Cries from over there!" Then he pointed at a building with a stepped gable at the far end of the square. "Looks like the Town Hall," the captain muttered. "Perhaps the burgomaster's woken up at last." He cupped his hands at his mouth and shouted, "Go and have a look, Urker! I'll come if you need me!"

The man on the back of the other ship waved and climbed back into his wheelhouse. The rusty hull of the UK 320 swung slowly round and crept toward the big building. Its top floor was out of the water, the big empty windows stared at them. Halfway across the square, the UK 320 suddenly shuddered and stopped. They could hear its bell ringing, white foam was thrashed up under its stern, but it didn't move. The captain muttered, "Aground? What the devil can that be?" He pulled the handle, the ship started to tremble again, and they crept slowly toward the gray hull in the center of the square. On its foredeck men with poles were furiously stabbing at something underneath the surface. "What is it?" the captain shouted, as they glided past. Someone on the foredeck of the UK 320 called back, "Don't know! It's concrete! Give us a rope, Urker!"

"In a minute!" the captain shouted back. "I'll go and have a look first! Be right back!" Then he turned toward the men out front and called, "Keep those poles going, Urkers! I'm going to pull alongside!" The cook called from the top of his galley, "Watch out—there may be a stoop in front!" The captain answered, "Aye," absently. He was suddenly different; a tense, hard man. He looked a real pirate now, about to board an enemy. As they drew nearer to the building, they heard cries: long wailing bleats, that sounded inhuman. The windows of the first floor were broken. When the ship edged near, the men craned their necks and looked inside. The captain muttered, "Hell!" Jan climbed onto their bench and saw a big room with a long green table, surrounded by high-backed armchairs. There were papers on the table, and ashtrays, and at the far end a blotter, a little hammer and a glass of water. Round the table trotted two white goats, bleating. The cook called to the wheelhouse, "Want them?" The captain shook his head and shouted, "I'll leave them to the Navy!" The bell rang, the ship trembled and backed away. Jan climbed slowly down again. He heard the bleating of the goats fade away, and tried to forget them.

They backed until they had come alongside the *UK 320*. "Still stuck?" the captain shouted. A man hollered back, "Aye! Give us a rope! It's the base of a bandstand!"

The men on the foredeck flung a rope at the back of the *UK 320*. The man from the wheelhouse caught it and made fast, "Ready?" the captain shouted. The man waved his arms over his head. The bell rang, the ship shivered and the children's vision became blurred as the racing engine rattled them. Then the bell rang again, the engine slowed and the captain shouted, "There you are, Urker! Get a move on!" The man unfastened the rope, it splashed in the water, foam came churning from underneath the *UK 320*'s stern once more and the ship swung back to the street they had been about to enter.

Then the captain became aware of the children again. He looked at them proudly and said, with a gesture toward the ship ahead, "Where would that Meter be without me to nurse him along? A bandstand! I ask you. What man ever put his ship onto a bandstand? But for us, people, this town would have had its monument, all ready and waiting, when the floods go down." Then he called to the cook, "Urker on the roof! Give these people a drink—and me a small one." As they sailed into the street, he sang "Mighty Lord Who Blasts Asunder, Death's Cold Silence with Thy Thunder."

The cook came with a small glass, and as he opened the door to the wheelhouse, he said to the children, "Don't listen to him. He makes them up as he goes along. Here you are, Urker."

The captain said, "Thank you, artist," and drank.

The village lay behind them, the poplars that had marked the road were gone. There was nothing now but a gray waste of water, with roofs in the distance, and nearby a muddy molehill on which two cows were huddled. Over the sea, the dark clouds sailed; far away on the horizon slanted a smoky curtain of rain.

The ships lunged on, rolling and pitching. The darkness of the rain came toward them like a net drawn across the water, passed over them, and as the net was drawn away, a beam of sunlight shone through the clouds and made a rainbow. It shimmered and grew until it made an arc in the grayness, as big as the world. The captain filled his pipe, gazing at the rainbow. Then the cook's voice called from out front, "Meter is going to the next one!"

The captain looked at the roof they were approaching, from which a white flag fluttered. The rusty hull of the *UK 320* ahead

[80]

of them was slowly swinging toward it. The captain pulled the handle, the bell rang and the ship slowed down.

The roof looked dead and lonely, a black pyramid of tiles, glistening with spray and rain. The waves lapped around it and there was nothing else in sight, not a tree, not a pole, not a piece of wreckage. As they came nearer they saw in the lee of the roof a triangular island of floating onions, caught there by the current and the wind.

The flag stuck out of a hole where a tile had been knocked off; it was a shirt, attached to a broomstick. The *UK 320* lowered a boat with two people inside; one man rowed, the other stood in the bow. The boat slowly edged its way round the roof into the island of onions; it moored alongside the guttering. The man in its bow started picking off roof tiles and throwing them in the water. Then he climbed onto the guttering, leaned on the roof, his legs spread, and looked through the hole he had made. He kicked off some more tiles, climbed up the cross-planks, stuck his legs into the hole, lowered himself and vanished.

The *UK 320* drifted past, rolling. When the hole came into view again, the man at the oars had climbed onto the guttering. A white bundle was handed to him from inside, and he let it drop into the boat. Then two white arms stretched out toward him from the hole; he took hold of them and lifted out a child in a nightshirt. He lowered the child carefully into the boat, took off his doublet and put it round the child's shoulders. His shirt was bright blue and fluttered in the wind. He put his arms into the hole once more and lifted out a second child, wrapped in a blanket.

When the other man finally came out, there were five children in the boat and two women, one of whom was hiding her face in her hands, her hair blown about. The other man took out a sewing machine, a bird cage, two more bundles and a basket with bottles; then two dark arms reached up toward him from the hole and he called the first man, who came to help him. Together they lifted out a man with a cap on and bare feet. After the man had been helped into the boat, one of the Urkers climbed higher up the roof, kicking off tiles, until he had reached the flagpole; he pulled it out and threw it into the water. The wind caught it as it fell, and blew out the shirt. It floated for a few seconds on the water like a pillow, then it vanished.

The boat was rowed slowly through the onions to the UK 320; the people from it were lifted on board by many hands, then the hooks were lowered, the men on the deck pulled the ropes, the boat rose dripping out of the water and the exhaust of the UK 320 started blowing black rings again. The UK 516 swung round, lurching, and headed for the next roof.

It was red and new, much bigger than the first one, and not shaped like a pyramid but gabled. Its white flag stuck from its chimney. It was a towel, tied to a stick. In the gable that faced them, there were two green doors. One of them swung open as they approached, but all it showed was darkness. "Man the boat!" the captain shouted. "I'll make a lee for you!" The cook called, "Aye!" and jumped off the galley.

The captain stood at the wheel again as he had when they approached the Town Hall. His jaw was set, his big hands clenched the spokes; he often pulled the handle, quickly, and the bell clanged. The ship drifted toward the house, cross-seas. The children had to cling onto the window sill so as not to fall, for they rolled worse than ever. When the gable of the house lay in the shelter of the ship, the captain shouted, "Let her go!" and pulleys squeaked as the boat was lowered. The captain rang the bell repeatedly now, and he spun the wheel one way or the other all the time. The engine raced, fell silent, raced; the ship lunged so wildly that Bussy started to whimper as he slid from side to side on the wheelhouse floor. "Lower the oil bags!" the captain shouted, and two men on the poop and the foredeck flung dripping sailcloth bags into the water, attached to a rope. The bags were full of holes and filled with cotton waste soaked in oil. As the men pulled them up and down in the water, a thin multicolored film spread over the waves in the trough of the ship, turning the gray, turbulent water into black marble, slowly heaving. The boat rowed toward the green door in the gable; the oars made shimmering rings as they dipped, the drops dripping from them drew orange and blue curves, that squirmed on the still black water. The ship shuddered and rattled as the engine raced, it rolled and clanked as it fell silent; the captain spun the wheel all the time and the few times he looked out to watch, he stood motionless, panting.

The cook and the old man with the hairy nose were in the boat. The old man rowed. When they hit the gable underneath the open door, the cook stood up and could be heard calling, "Come on out, people, or you'll have the ship on your roof!"

But no one came. The wind caught the door and slammed it shut. The cook took an oar and hammered on the door, but no one opened it. Then he stuck the edge of the oar in a crack and levered the door open. It slammed back against the wall with a crash. The cook waited until the slow swell of the black water had lifted the boat once more, then he jumped, grabbed the threshold, and scrambled inside. He had just landed on his knees, the pale soles of his clogs were all that could be seen of him in the darkness, when the wind caught the door again and slammed it shut.

After that, nothing seemed to happen. The engine raced and stopped, the captain spun the wheel, the boat rose and fell slowly up and down the gable with the lonely man inside. Every time the black water fell, the strip of wall where it had been gleamed like mother-of-pearl, as if reflecting the washed-out colors of the broken arc of the rainbow that rose behind the roof. The captain finally gave a blast on the siren, that echoed back from the gable and skimmed away across the water. Then the door opened again and the cook looked out, shouting something at the man below. The engine was racing just then, so his words could not be heard. The man in the boat stooped and handed up a lantern. The cook took it inside; the little flame vanished in the darkness.

This time the cook came back more quickly. The engine had fallen silent and the ship lay rolling slowly, when he appeared in the doorway once more. He put down the lantern at his feet and shouted between his hands, "Seventeen! All dead! What do we do?" The captain stood silent for a moment, then he shouted, "Leave them! Come back!" The bell clanged again, the engine raced, he spun the wheel, while the cook handed down the lantern and lowered himself until he hung from the threshold. As the boat rose, he fell, and slumped on the bench. The old man pushed the boat off with an oar, then he rowed back, making shimmering rings on the still black water. As the boat's bow cleaved the swell, it drew colored ribbons after it, that swiftly faded.

"Hook her!" the captain shouted. The pulleys squeaked as the blocks soared down. When the boat rose from the water, the bell clanged and the trembling ship swung away, its engine racing. The green door was caught by the wind again, and slammed shut once more, but the sound could not be heard.

As Jan looked back, he saw the colors vanish in the wake of the ship. The waves nearest the house still shimmered blue and orange for a little while, then all was gray again. The cook came to the wheelhouse and said through the window, "I can't understand that. All lying close together. How could they have died?"

The captain shrugged his shoulders. "Exposure," he said, "or perhaps the first wave drowned them."

The cook nodded, then he asked, "Want some gin?"

The captain shook his head. "But you go ahead," he said.

"I think I will," said the cook, and he ambled off, dragging his clogs.

"How is it that the bottoms of his clogs are white?" Jan asked.

The captain turned round and looked down at him, frowning. Then his face became kind again, and he said, "That's because the paint wore off, and the sea has bleached them." He looked at Adinda, who sat staring at her hands, her head bent; he left the wheel, put out a hand toward her, lifted her chin, said, "Never mind," and kissed her. Then he went back to the wheel again.

The ship was heading for a cluster of roofs, from all of which white flags were fluttering. Against the chimney of one of them, a dark shape huddled. As they came nearer, they saw it was a woman, wrapped in a blanket. In front of her lay a small body across the rooftop, on its stomach, its arms dangling.

"Well, children," the captain said, "I think you'd better go back to the galley. It's cold up here." He lowered a window and called, "Cook!" As the cook's head appeared, he called, "Come and get the children!"

The cook came, and lifted them out of the wheelhouse. His breath now smelled of petrol too. He took them by the hand, led them back to the galley and put them on the little bench again. Then he stepped inside himself, and called to the wheelhouse, "I'll stick with my pans now, Urker!" The captain's voice

[85]

answered, "Aye!" and the cook shut the door, plunging the galley in darkness. A match scraped; he lifted the flame in his cupped hands to a little oil lamp that hung rattling on the wall. As he lit the wick, the flame smoked, for the glass was broken. The bell rang in the depths, the engine fell silent and outside the captain's voice shouted, "Let her go!" There was the sound of clogs on the iron deck, and the squeaking of pulleys. Then Bussy scrambled at the door, yelping. The cook opened up and lifted him inside. Bussy went toward the stove, ignoring Ko and Noisette, who huddled in the far corner, snoozing. He sat down at the oven door and looked up, his head on one side, his right ear cocked. "Ah," said the cook. "So you like my fish? Well, good for you." He took another grimy plate out of the stove, put it down and said, "Remember what we decided? Sea dogs don't burn their noses." As Bussy cautiously sniffed, there came from outside the sound of a high voice, screaming. "I know!" said Cook. "While he sits waiting for his fish to cool, we'll teach him to sing. Do you know 'My Mother Had a Mermaid's Tail'?"

The children shook their heads.

"Ah," said the cook, "that's a beauty. Every child from Urk knows it. But you must join in after each line with 'Hi ho,' like this . . ." He closed his eyes and sang, "Hi ho!" with a swing of his head. "Here goes: 'My mother had a mermaid's tail . . .' Well?"

"Hi, ho," said Jan, flatly.

"No," said the cook, "sing! Here we go again: 'My mother had a mermaid's tail . . .' "

Jan opened his mouth to sing "Hi ho," when the voice screamed again outside. Adinda began to cry.

The cook rubbed his chin and said, "Well, not being from Urk, I don't suppose you're musical. Now let's see. It's about

[86]

time to start cooking the meal. Hey, you, little lady. Can you make pancakes?"

Adinda did not answer. She sat forlorn in her corner, her face in her hands, crying. The cook knelt in front of her, upsetting the plate of fish with one of his clogs. "I asked whether you can make pancakes," he said gruffly. "What about an answer?"

Adinda shook her head, without taking her hands away. "Well," said the cook. "Let me teach you. Come on! We start by making the batter." He took hold of her wrists to pull her hands away, but she shook her head again, and Bussy started yapping at the bits of fish that slithered on the floor as the ship rolled. The cook looked down, saw the mess he had made, sighed, put out his hand for support to get to his feet, touched the stove, cried "Ouch!" and sucked his fingers. Then he scrambled to his feet, took a swig from the bottle, and poured some of it onto his fingers. The engine bell clanged, the ship started shaking again; he held out one finger to Adinda. "Here," he said, "taste this, it's medicine, just for the two of us. Here!" Adinda shook her head. The cook rubbed his chin again, then he took a tin from the shelf, put a lump of sugar on the palm of his hand, poured medicine over it and held it out to Adinda. "Eat this, little heart," he said. "Then we're going to make pancakes and help one another, for that's what we need, you and me."

Adinda took the sugar and sucked it. Jan looked at her enviously and puckered his face. The cook said, "I see you coming, boy, from a long, long way off. Well, all right." He soaked another lump of sugar and gave it to Jan, who munched it in a manly fashion, but his mouth got so hot that he had to keep it open, and tears sprang to his eyes.

"You see," said the cook, "it won't work for those who don't need it. Now you'll be sick."

Jan shook his head. "More," he said.

[87]

"Don't ask for more," said the cook, "for you won't get it. You're a big boy, you don't need any medicine. All right, we make the batter."

He took a pan off the shelf and started pouring things into it. Outside, voices hollered and the engine raced and stopped all the time. The galley became very hot, the smell of soot and fish made Jan feel sick. The ship went on rolling, the pans on the stove slid to and fro; every time they stopped, there was a hissing sound. Bussy gave up eating and waddled toward the far corner, skidding on the slippery fish. "Hook her!" the captain's voice shouted outside. The pulleys squeaked. "Here you are," said the cook, holding out the bowl with a wooden spoon in it, "beat this." Adinda hesitated, then she took the bowl. "That's the girl," said the cook. "Here, here's a prize for you." He soaked another lump of sugar; she opened her mouth as he held it out to her, and he popped it in. Then he said musingly, "Now what can you do, boy?" Outside, the captain's voice shouted, "Watch out! Hold back that woman!" Clogs scurried along the deck, and there was a scream again, very near. "I know!" said the cook, "while she makes the pancakes, we'll cut the bread. Can you do that?"

"Oh yes," said Jan. "I've got a knife of my own. Look!" and he hitched out of the pocket of his apron the penknife the bos'n had given him that morning. "Fine," said the cook. "Now where the hell is the bread?" The engine bell rang out and everything rattled as the ship lurched and reared. Adinda clutched her bowl and put her feet against the rail of the stove. "Well, never mind," said the cook, "we'll cut the bread later. Do you know the story of the three whalers who loved the same girl?" Jan shook his head, burping. "Ah," said the cook, lifting a grimy finger. "It's the most beautiful story ever to come out of Urk. They were called Jan, Jonah and Jeroen, and each of them had a ship, three beautiful whalers called the *Sea-flame*, the *Sea-star* and the *Sea-flower*. One evening, when they came back from a three years' trip, their ships full of barrels of oil and crates of ambergris . . ." Adinda started to hum as she briskly whipped the batter, and Jan said, "I want to be sick." The cook blew out his cheeks, scratched his head and said, "Well, I think you'd better lie down on that bench for a while. You'll see, that'll make you feel better." Jan lay down, heaving, his eyes closed; Adinda sang "All Ye Prisoners Arise," beating time as she whipped. "God," said the cook, "have mercy on me, miserable sinner," then he sat down on the edge of the bench, his head in his hands.

The door was opened, letting in a gust of wind, and the flame smoked. It was the old man with the hairy nose. "Hot water, Urker," he said. "Here comes another one."

The cook looked up, said, "On the stove. Help yourself. You be midwife this time." The old man said, "Aye," and took a pan. "No," said the cook. "Not that one, that's soup. And don't say no one will notice the difference, I'm sick of it." The old man shrugged his shoulders, took another pan and lifted it carefully over Adinda's legs. Before he shut the door behind him, he said, "Better put some more on, Urker. The day is young."

"Well?" asked Adinda, when they were alone once more. "What do I do next?"

The cook said, "I'll show you," and he taught her how to make pancakes while Jan slept on the bench, and the boat was lowered and raised many times, and the pans slid to and fro on the stove, hissing. An hour later, he cautiously opened the door of the galley, threw a bucket of pancakes overboard, tiptoed back to the galley and cautiously closed the door again.

[89]

Three hours later, the ship anchored. The bell clanged for the last time, the engine stopped, and the old man with the hairy nose opened the galley door once more. "Come on out, Urker," he said, "we're through for the day. Tide's running low, we can't get out for the next six hours."

The cook said, "Ssh!" pointing at the bench, and then he asked in a whisper, "How many?"

"Sixty-five," the old man said, "and the baby is a girl. What about something to eat?"

The cook sighed. "All right," he said. "Bring up a barrel of fish."

The old man shuffled away. As the cook stood staring at the broken dike, the floating wreckage, the dead cattle, and the billowing field of onions in which fourteen ships lay anchored around them, Adinda's voice asked from the galley behind him, "Where are the pancakes?"

The cook turned round and answered, "Eaten, child, eaten. Did you sleep well?"

"Eaten by whom?" Adinda asked.

The cook said, "By the captain, child."

"Did he like them?"

The cook said, "Yes."

The captain came clumping along the deck, scratching his waist by turning his trousers. "Well, Urker," he said, "while you sat on your arse in the galley, we saved sixty-five souls."

The cook said, "Good."

A rumbling noise approached, the old man with the hairy nose called, "Gangway!" and rolled a barrel to the galley door. As the cook stooped, the captain said, "Well—another woman, born in the island of Urk."

The cook belched, and heaved in the fish.

When the children woke up, the sun was setting. They woke up because of a tremendous roar in the sky. As they looked out of the galley door with the cook, they saw a vast arrowhead of airplanes fly overhead toward the red fire of the setting sun, black birds against the sky. On the deck were many strange people: women and children and dogs and goats. They all looked up at the sky, and listened. Then the cook took a pan, beat it with a spoon and called, "Down into the hold, people! Food's coming!"

Four sailors came to fetch the two huge laundry bins in which the fish had been cooked, and carried them to the bulkhead of the hold. Then the boom of the foremast was swung over, the bins were hooked in a pulley, one by one, and lowered into the hold. The cook said, "Come on, children. Mealtime," and took them by the hand.

As they arrived at the bulkhead and looked down into the

hold, they saw a tight crowd of people standing, squatting and lying close together in disorder among bundles, wireless sets, bird cages and suitcases. Many women held babies, and there were cats and little dogs too. Torches flamed along the walls, spluttering and smoking. The sailors moved among the crowd, handing out white wash basins filled with fish, one to each family. The cook said to Jan, "You wait here, I'll come back for you," then he took Adinda in his arms and climbed down the Jacob's ladder with her. He carried her through the crowd to where the captain sat between two lanterns, on top of a stack of barrels, a book on his lap. He came back for Jan and carried him to the captain too. Downstairs was a sickening smell of sweat and mud and wet clothing; the smoke of the torches billowed up in black rolling clouds through the open hatch, whenever the wind blew in the flames flattened, the smoke swirled down and added the stench of soot. The captain called, "Christians! The Bible!" and the hubbub of voices fell silent. In a corner, a small child went on crying, like a lost lamb. The captain opened the book on his lap, put on a pair of steel-rimmed spectacles and read.

"Ye are the children of the Lord, your God . . . Thou shalt not eat any abominable thing . . . These ye shall eat of all that are in the waters: all that have fins and scales shall ye eat: And whatsoever hath not fins and scales ye may not eat; it is unclean unto you. Of all clean birds ye shall eat, but these are they of which ye shall not eat: the eagle, and the ossifrage, and the ospray; and the glede, and the kite, and the vulture after his kind, and every raven after his kind, and the owl and the night hawk and the cuckoo, and the hawk after his kind, the little

[92]

owl and the great owl and the swan, and the pelican and the gier eagle, and the cormorant, and the stork, and the heron after her kind, and the lapwing, and the bat. And every creeping thing that flieth is unclean to you: they shall not be eaten.

"Ye shall not eat of anything that dieth of itself: thou shalt give it unto the stranger that is in thy gates, that he may eat it; or thou mayest sell it unto an alien; for thou art an holy people unto the Lord thy God. Thou shalt not seethe a kid in his mother's milk. . . .

"And thou shalt eat before the Lord thy God, in the place which He shall choose to place his name there."

The captain closed the Bible, took off his spectacles, closed his eyes and folded his hands. "Lord of the damned and the broken," he said, "Thou hast written: where two or three are gathered together in my name, there I am, in the midst of them. So we salute thee. Amen."

The baby had gone on crying all the time; at the captain's feet a woman had started to sob, and now an older one comforted her, stroking her hair. "All right, people," the captain said, "eat and enjoy yourselves. This fish has been cooked by the best cook in the island of Urk." There was a silence, then a man's voice asked from the darkness, "Aren't there any forks?" There was a great hubbub of voices, and the captain said, "Use the forks God gave you, people, as we have done all our lives." A woman said, "God bless you, sailor. Without you . . ." then she burst into tears. "All right," said the captain, "now let's all stop sighing and crying and enjoy our food while it's hot. After the meal, the tide will have come up high enough for us to sail through the breach in the dike, back into the open. In some hours' time you'll all be in Bruinisse, where there are hospital ships with baths, doctors, clothes and everything."

A young man, surrounded by little children, asked, "What will they do with us then?"

"They'll take you to Rotterdam or to Dordrecht or to Bergen op Zoom," the captain said, "and from there on, you'll be put up with people inland, until the dikes are mended and your fields and your houses are dry again."

"But why did you—did they take so long taking us off?" asked a thin woman, who was wearing a man's hat. "We've been sitting on our roofs for four days and four nights. At least two people have died because you left us so long."

"At least two thousand people have died," the captain said, "and there are many more missing."

"Nonsense," said the woman. "There were only six hundred people in the polder."

"But there were hundreds of thousands in the other polders," the captain said. "One fifth of Holland has been flooded. Look at us, Urkers—we sailed with three hundred ships. The fourteen lying around us now are the biggest fleet I've seen since the day we sailed into these islands, and it's not only us Urkers who have come to take you off your roofs. There's the Volendammers, the Spakenburgers, the Elburgers, the fleets from Ymuiden, Scheveningen and Katwijk. There's the Navy, and all the yachts and small boats of Holland; there's the French, the Italians, the Americans, the Danes, the English, the Germans, the Belgians, with ships and flying machines and floating automobiles. Have you seen them? Neither have I. This land is as big as the sea now, and that we have found you at all is a miracle of God. Your houses were at least left standing, for you to sit on top of; all around you whole villages have been swept away by a tidal wave that smashed the houses and killed every living soul inside. So eat your food, be grateful and shut up."

"Did the Navy send you?" the same voice asked that had asked about the forks.

The captain shut his eyes; then he answered, "No one has sent us. We, who know the sea, said when we heard of what had happened to you: there, but for the Grace of God, go we. So let's remember the dead, and eat."

Then an old woman got to her feet. She looked huge and terrifying with her vast bulk in a red blanket, rubber hip boots that had sagged down her legs, and white hair, smeared with mud and caked on her forehead. "Christian," she said, "the hand of the Lord is upon your shoulder. For, what He said to the fishermen of the Dead Sea two thousand years ago, He has fulfilled tonight: 'Follow me, fishermen,' He said, 'and I'll make you fishers of men.' You were right: here He is, in the midst of us, and I see Him in your eyes."

The captain scratched his head, pushed his cap over his eyebrows and said, "Thank you, Mother. You tell 'em to eat."

The big woman looked round the hold in a deep silence; then she sat down, and they ate.

The children were not hungry, and after they had sat toying with their food for a while, sleep overcame them. They drowsed until the meal was over; then the cook carried them back to the galley and there they fell asleep again on the bench.

When they woke up for the second time, the ship was at sea. It was night. Outside the galley, a green light was shining that rose and fell with the swell, crossing the silver streak of the horizon. The cook gave them a blanket each to wrap around their shoulders against the cold night wind that blew in from the sea, then he said: "Come and look at Bruinisse." They came out on deck and stood staring at the sky, leaning closely together against the warm wall of the galley. They were too small and the ship's bow was too high for them to see the horizon ahead; all they saw were two tremendous beams of searchlights, lighting up the clouds. Above them, red, green and white lights winked, drifting swiftly through the darkness. "Those are planes," the cook said, "on their way to drop things in isolated places."

"What do they drop?" Jan asked.

"Food and blankets and rubber boats and bottles of gas," the cook said. "Also bags to put sand in, to mend the dikes. Those searchlights shine on the clouds so that their reflection may give the men working on the dikes some light."

"We saw them working on the dike from the belfry," Jan said, "but one of the lorries was washed away, and so were all the sandbags."

"Where was that?" the cook asked.

"Niewerland," said Jan.

The cook said nothing.

As they neared the land, the big silhouette of a warship loomed up against the sky. On its bridge, a little light flickered nervously. The cook turned to the wheelhouse and shouted, "The Navy's signaling!" The captain's voice answered, "Aye." They passed more warships, six of them, black and colossal against the false dawn of the searchlights. Then a red and a green light came speeding toward them, and the roar of an engine; a ghostly launch swerved in the distance and slowed down. A metallic voice hailed them and bellowed, "All fishing smacks moor in the port of refuge, north of the pierhead, and report to the Port Authority!"

The cook looked at the wheelhouse, but no answer came forth.

A searchlight stabbed at them, played along their hull, then the metallic voice bellowed, "*UK 516! UK 516!* Have you heard me? Have you heard me?"

As still no answer came from the wheelhouse, the cook sighed and shook his head. The distant engine spurted, the launch lifted its bow and came snarling toward them. As the angry white mustache of its bow wave flashed in the darkness, the cook said, "Lord, now he's got the bit in his teeth." The launch looked as if it were going to ram them, then it swerved at a right angle, and lay alongside. From a small glass wheelhouse an officer emerged, very young in the green light. "Why don't you answer?" he called, in a small natural voice this time.

The cook leaned over the rail and said kindly, "Never mind. We know where to go. We've been here before."

"Next time you're hailed, please acknowledge," the officer said stiffly. "And now do as you are told!"

"Next time you see an Urker, leave him alone," said the cook. "I say this for your own good. We're all very tired, we haven't slept for four nights. . . ."

Then the captain opened the wheelhouse, jumped to the rail, and as his clogs hit the deck with a clatter, he shouted, "Piss off!"

The young officer, rising and falling with the swell, cried, "I beg your pardon?"

The captain screamed, "Piss off, you little bloodsucker, or I'll smash you!" Then he sprang back into the wheelhouse.

The cook said hastily, "Better leave him, boy. Don't worry." Then the bell clanged, the ship shuddered, the engine raced, and the *UK 516* swung round, pushing the launch sideways. The officer lost his balance and slipped, clinging to the hand line, shouting, "Astern! Astern!" The engine of the launch

[97]

roared and it tried to back away, but the *UK 516* shoved it sideways with such pressure that it was helpless. While nervous shouts and curses came from alongside, the captain forced the launch to make the full turn of the compass before he finally released it. As it drifted slowly off, an anxious voice called in the distance, "Sir! Sir! The rudder's damaged!" The cook scratched his head and muttered, "That's what comes of telling him that God shines from his eyes."

"Why was the captain angry?" Jan asked.

"Because he's been wanting to be angry all day," said the cook. "He needs it for his constitution."

"And why was the Navy angry?"

"Because the Navy's ships draw too much water to enter the flooded land," the cook said, "so all they can do is organize the ships that come out."

"I didn't like that officer," Jan said. "He looked like a policeman."

"Well, that's what they are just now," the cook said. "And you don't become a policeman to make civilians love you."

"I liked him," said Adinda calmly.

"That," said the cook, "is why people join the Navy."

The captain called from the wheelhouse, "Man the fenders, I'm going to moor over starboard!"

The cook muttered, "That's the first time I've heard him talk about fenders. He must have scared himself as well." The old man with the hairy nose called from the foredeck, "Ain't no fenders, Urker! What d'you want 'em for?"

"To save the paint of the hospital ship!" the captain called out, "and mind your own business!"

"There ain't no paint left on the hospital ship," the old man called back. "You scraped her clean last time."

[98]

"Shut up!" the captain shouted; then the bell clanged, the ship slowed down and swung into the harbor.

At first the harbor seemed very small, just a narrow patch of water surrounded by a forest of masts. Then, as the ship turned round, searchlights groped for it from the shore and, by their very distance, the size of the port was revealed. It was very big, much bigger than any port the children had ever seen, and crammed with hundreds of ships. Fishing smacks from all the harbors of Holland, big yachts with high masts, a mail steamer with scores of shining portholes, two gray warships with a fleet of small gray boats alongside. The *UK 516* slowly edged toward a plump, white sailing barge with rounded bows and lee-boards. It had a swept-up roof and big windows, from which yellow light was shining. From a tall pole on the crown of its rudder, a white flag with a red cross fluttered.

The captain gave three short blasts on the siren, and people came out on the aftdeck of the barge. One of them was a buxom young woman in a blue dress with a white apron. The captain opened the door of the wheelhouse and shouted at the barge, "Customers for you!"

The woman called back, "What is it this time?"

"All children!" the captain shouted. "Two strays, one sick, and a new-born baby!"

"How old?" the woman called.

"Six hours!" the captain shouted; then the bell clanged, the engine raced and the *UK 516* slowly backed alongside the white barge. Ropes thumped on the deck, and the cook said, "Well, children, let's get the animals. You're going."

"But I don't want to go," Jan said, frightened.

"And I'm sorry you're going," the cook said, "but you must, boy. We'll hand you over to these nice people here, then we take the rest over to that big steamer and then we sail back through the dike again to get the next lot. You'll see; you'll have a wonderful time on board that hospital ship. It's full of toys."

"I don't want any toys," Jan said tearfully. "I want to stay with you."

"Hush," said the cook. "Next time we're in, we'll all come to see you. Bussy, Bussy!" Bussy came scampering toward him, and stood up against the high threshold of the galley, wagging his tail. Ko and Noisette stared at him from their far corner. "Kitty, Kitty," the cook called, but Noisette did not move. So he lifted Bussy by the scruff of his neck, handed him to Jan, stepped inside to pick up Noisette, but the moment he stretched out his hand, she jumped onto the shelf. "Kitty, Kitty," the cook said, groping behind the pans. Noisette's head peeped out a yard away, and the cook said, "Ah! There you are." But when he put out his hand to catch her, she vanished behind the pans again, and they clattered all down the row. Jan called, anxiously, "Noisette, Noisette, we're going away! Come on, quick!" Ko hopped placidly toward the door. The cook parted his legs to let him pass, then he started rattling the pans on the shelf. Noisette peeped out again, behind his back, and Adinda climbed onto the bench to get her. But Noisette jumped on top of a pan, and started delicately walking along the top of the row, her short tail stuck up. The cook saw her coming, turned over the last pan in the row, stealthily took a lid and hid it behind his back. Noisette stood still on top of the last pan but one, cocked her head and looked at him. He called sweetly, "Come, come! Pst! Pst!" But Noisette just stood there, looking innocent, thrashing her tail. Then the cook jumped. There was a loud clatter, and a crash as the bench toppled over;

the cook lay sprawled among his pans in front of the stove, and Noisette had shot out of the door into the night. Adinda cried, "Noisette! Noisette!" but the kitten had vanished in the darkness.

The cook scrambled to his feet, and as he stood rubbing his knee he said, "Come along, children. You must go now."

"But Noisette!" Jan cried. "We can't go without Noisette! Please, please don't let us go without Noisette!"

"Never mind," said the cook. "I'll look after her, and I'll give her to you when we come back."

Then Adinda suddenly started to cry. "You won't come back," she sobbed. "You won't ever come back. We'll never see Noisette again."

"God," said the cook, "have mercy." He gave Ko to Adinda, put his hands on their shoulders, and pushed the children toward the gate in the rail where the captain and the woman with the white apron stood waiting.

Jan tried to back away, also crying now, and Adinda convulsively sobbed into Ko's neck. The cook growled, "Come along, come along," as Jan struggled to get away and kicked and screamed. Then the woman stepped onto the deck, said, "Stop it, children, no nonsense," picked up Adinda and Ko under her right arm, Jan and Bussy under her left, and carried them off. Jan was so taken aback that he forgot to struggle; as she stepped across onto the other deck, the captain said admiringly, "Well, Sister, we must have a romp sometime."

"Not even if you soaked yourself in soda for a week first," she said. "How is your leg?"

"My leg," said the captain, "is doing fine."

The sister shook her head. "If you had let me bandage those

sores," she said, "instead of putting your dirty underpants back on again, they would have healed by now."

"I don't want them healed," the captain said. "I'm used to them."

"All right," the woman said, "as long as everybody's happy. Well, good-by."

"Good-by, mighty Sister," the captain said. "When I'm wandering on the waters again, I'll sing a psalm about you."

The cook said, "Watch out, Sister," and the captain turned on him angrily. "Watch out for what, you blob of slime?" he demanded.

"Watch out for the rope," the cook said. "Your ship is leaving." Then he slammed shut the gate in the rail and Jan, recovered, started to cry again, "Noisette! Noisette!" as the dark rusty ship moved away. The woman hugged him, said, "Hush! Don't cry." Then she called, "Who's Noisette?"

The cook shouted back, "A cat!" and then, all of a sudden, there was Noisette, perched on the rail of the *UK* 516. Before Jan could cry her name once more, she had arched her back and jumped. She caught the rail of the barge with the tips of her claws, hung for a moment in agonizing suspense, then she swung herself onto the deck, strolled casually toward them, and rubbed her head against the sister's leg.

"Well," she said. "Look who's here!" and she put the children down. "Now what about waving good-by to the captain? Quick! They're going!"

Jan, still heaving, waved lamely at the vanishing ship. The captain and the cook waved back. "Come on," the sister said to Adinda. "You wave too. Here, give me that toy," and she stretched out her hand toward Ko, who had hung motionlessly all the time, his eyes shut, his hind legs dangling. When she took him over she said, "Christmas!" and dropped him. Ko hopped away, kicking out his left hind leg. Adinda waved and cried, "Good-by!" From across the water came the captain's voice that boomed, "Good-by, little Negro! If you ever feel lost, come to the island of Freedom!"

Jan cried, "Good-by! Good-by!" too, but the engine of the UK 516 was racing now and the captain just waved. Then, as the ship swung round and the children went on waving, the big woman with white hair who had spoken during the meal waved back, and all the others on the deck joined her. It was so unexpected, and such a wonderful moment, that Jan tugged at the sister's sleeve and said, breathlessly, "Did you see that? They all waved at me! Everybody!"

"Well, so they should," the sister said. "It must have been nice to have you on board. We're lucky to have you. Come, we'll go and have some cocoa."

The barge, that had looked clumsy and old-fashioned from the outside, was on the inside a comfortable modern apartment. It had obviously been converted hastily into a hospital ship, for behind the tiers of bunks in the main cabin were the big windows, with flower pots still on the sills, and on the walls there were pictures and ships in bottles. In the entrance stood a couple of children's scooters; below the ordinary coat rack was a second one, much lower down, decorated with red-capped dwarfs and Donald Ducks. The ship had electric lighting, mainly from table lamps with frilly shades, a bathroom with hot and cold water and a children's seat in the lavatory. It had central heating and a model kitchen, in which a grimy old man in a short white coat was now pottering. A diesel generating plant hummed on the foredeck, an electric pump for the water pressure switched on and off automatically underneath the floor of the dining room, while the children sat drinking their cocoa from paper mugs. On the dining-room wall hung a big photograph of the ship as it must have looked before the floods: just like a house, full of easy chairs, low tables and rugs, showing two parents and three small children, gazing hostilely at the camera.

Jan and Adinda were taken to bed in a small room in the back of the ship. It was lined with books and had a desk in it. On the desk stood a big black machine full of lamps that zoomed softly; a loudspeaker droned monotonous messages. A thin young man with a big nose and little blue eyes very close together sat biting his nails in an armchair, his feet on the table. As the children were brought in by the sister, the loudspeaker droned, ". . . on each pierhead, and five torches delining the area where the canisters are to be dropped. I repeat: a message for the burgomaster of Stavenisse, Stavenisse, from the Territorial Commander District Five: aircraft will drop twenty canisters with food and five hundred blankets at twenty-two hours thirty, twenty-two hundred thirty. Please put one fire on each pierhead. . . ."

"Here are two guests for you, Sparks," Sister said. "I'm going to put them in the lower bunk."

The young man took his finger out of his mouth and raised his invisible eyebrows. "You're mad, sweetheart," he said, "he'll be back at zero thirty."

"I don't know what you're talking about," the sister said curtly, "but if he comes back, send him to me. They may come for the corpse any minute; after that I'll have a bunk for him."

The young man said, "Charming."

"And that's not all," Sister said. "Here come some more." She made a kissing noise and Bussy came scampering in, his ears flopping. "There's a cat and a rabbit too," she continued, "and they are all going to sleep in Mr. Tadema's bunk."

The young man said, "What? No crocodile?"

The sister patted him on the head and said, "Isn't it lovely to sit in a chair with your feet on the table, picking your nose and sticking it under the seat, and have the time to think of witty answers?"

"You seem to think that I'm just . . ." the young man began, but the sister interrupted him by saying: "That's right. Now, come on, children. In you go." She uncovered the lower of the two bunks that were let into the wall. On a panel by the side of a narrow door with a ventilator, a green light flashed on. Then there was a soft hissing noise, a swoosh, and a quivering roar came from behind the door. "Don't worry about that," the sister said as Jan backed away. "It's the automatic oil burner for the central heating. Now, I think you're going to put your head against the wall, what's your name. . . ."

"Adinda."

"You put your head against the wall, Adinda, and the little boy at the other end, and don't kick one another or Sparks will get angry. As you can see, he's very busy."

The young man made a coarse gesture, the radio droned, "Here is a message for the water tank ship *Rotterdam Sixteen*. Please proceed at once to the harbor of Onderkerk, Onderkerk, which can be entered at high tide only. A pilot will be waiting for you at Buoy Seven A, Buoy Seven A, acknowledge Scheveningen radio. I repeat, Here is a message for the water tank ship *Rotterdam Sixteen*. . . ."

"These people are marvelous," the young man said. "Buoy Seven A, indeed. They seem to be the only ones who don't know there isn't a single buoy left in the area."

"I am sure everything would go much better if you were sitting in Headquarters," the sister said, taking off Jan's apron. "They would certainly go much better here."

"I have the growing impression," the young man said, looking at his nails, "that you are nurturing . . ." A voice in the corridor called, "Sister! Sister, are you there?"

The sister called, "Yes!"

The doctor appeared in the doorway, looking like a butcher in his smeared white coat. "An open fracture of the tibia has just come in," he said. "I need you for a transfusion."

"Ah," said Sister to the wireless operator, "now here's your chance, young man. You undress those children and put them to bed. You wash their teeth, faces and hands, put on these pajamas, fold their clothes, put them neatly away, and then you read a chapter of this book to them."

The young man held the dog-eared book at arm's length and looked at it with an expression of distaste. "*Adventures in a Haystack,*" he read out. "What is this? Your memoirs?"

"Come on, Sister," the doctor said. "Your answer can wait."

The sister kissed the children, and said, "Good night, dears. Be nice and quiet, I'll come to see you in the morning."

"Where are Ko and Noisette?" Jan asked as she went to the door.

"They are finishing their meal," she said. "Cook will bring them along in a minute."

"Here's a message from the burgomaster of Zierikzee," the radio intoned, "for all shallow vessels in the area. The top floor of the Municipal Hospital has now become untenable and the patients are being carried to the roof. Assistance is urgently required. I repeat, here is a message from the burgomaster . . ."

"Well, children," the young man said, "let me see how quickly you can undress. The one who is in bed first gets this," and he held up a silver wireless valve. Jan started to undress at once; Adinda remained where she was, sitting on the edge of the bunk, her hands in her lap.

"Doesn't this tempt you?" the young man asked, holding out the valve to her. "You can tie it on a string and hang it round your neck. Very smart, in New Guinea."

Adinda said nothing.

The young man smiled, waggling his ears, and turned the valve to make it flash in the lamplight. Then he said "Ah! I know!" opened a drawer without taking his feet off the table and brought out a pink quill. "A beautiful feather to stick in your bonnet," he said. "It can do with a bit of gaiety, I feel."

Adinda answered in her flat voice, "I don't want to stick a feather in my bonnet."

"Well," said the young man, "if you undress quickly, it's yours, and you can stick it wherever you like."

Jan laughed.

"Ah," said the young man, grinning, "a fellow wit, I see." Then slouching steps came along the corridor, and the grimy old man in the white coat appeared, carrying Ko and Noisette. He looked tired and long-suffering, and said, "When Mr. Tadema comes back, I must talk to him. Either they leave, or I will."

"And who might 'they' be?" the young man inquired.

"Those bloody women," Cook answered. "Do you know the latest?"

The radio droned, "Here is a message from the burgomaster of Onderkerk concerning coffins. . . ."

"Creepers," said Cook. "How can you sit here and listen to that sinister stuff, grinning from ear to ear?"

The young man shrugged his shoulders. "I suppose you get used to anything," he said, "after listening to it for twenty-four hours a day for four days running."

"I suppose you don't hear it any more," Cook said, "so what's the use of having it on?"

"Don't you worry," the young man answered. "If there's a message for us, I'll hear it all right. Now tell me the latest about those bloody women."

"Aw," Cook said. "Never mind."

". . . so no more coffins, please," the radio droned, "no more coffins, please. Ships carrying coffins to Onderkerk should alter course for Stavenisse, where they are urgently needed."

"It's incredible," the young man said. "They asked for three hundred in Onderkerk and four different authorities obliged, so they've got twelve hundred by now. You won't be able to see what's left of the village for coffins."

"Creepers," said Cook.

"Urgent," the radio droned, "urgent, urgent. Message from the Territorial Commander, District Five, to all evacuation vessels proceeding empty toward any destination. Previous orders canceled. All converge at top speed on Zurland Estuary, Zurland Estuary . . ."

"I'm in bed!" Jan called. "Look, mister, I'm in bed."

"Splendid," said the young man. "Give the gentleman this valve, Cook. And my name is Sparks."

"Where do you want me to put these animals?" Cook asked. "With him?"

"Yes," said Sparks. "All converge on the captain's bunk; urgent message from Head Sister."

"Want some more cocoa, kiddies?" Cook asked, dumping the animals between them. "If you like, I'll let you have another mug."

Jan said, "Yes, please." Adinda shook her head.

"Shouldn't you undress?" Cook asked her. "Or are you bothered by the presence of us gentlemen?"

Adinda said nothing.

"All right," said Cook. "I'll take a sheet and hold it in front of you. Get a move on."

He took a sheet from the top bunk, spread it out behind his back and turned round to screen Adinda.

The loudspeaker said, ". . . not to sail into the flooded area under any circumstances. I repeat: the Butane ships *Shell Five* and *Shell Seven* are not to sail into the flooded area under any circumstances. End of message."

"Ah," said Sparks. "They've copped it at last! Do you know that those Butane ships have been sailing in through the gaps in the dike of their own accord, to hand out bottles of gas to stranded people? I have been waiting for this. They draw at least six feet."

The cook, standing with his arms spread, holding the sheet behind him, like an inventor about to fly, asked, "Where's Mr. Tadema gone, by the way?"

"To Onderkerk, with a Y-boat of the Navy," Sparks said. "It seems they may be wanting us there. Over two hundred dead, and the harbor entrance draws four feet at high tide. We are the only hospital ship that can get in."

"All right, kiddie," Cook said over his shoulder. "Are you in bed?" He lowered the sheet and looked round.

Adinda still sat on the edge of the bunk, her hands in her lap, fully dressed. "Hey!" he said. "What are you waiting for?"

Adinda looked up at him calmly, and said, "I'm not sleepy."

As the cook seemed at a loss for an answer, Sparks said, "Come on, sweetheart, go to bed or we'll get into trouble with Sister. And don't expect me to humor you, you'll have to be grown up for once. I hate baby talk."

Adinda said, "I want to go home."

"Where is that?" Sparks asked, putting his feet on the table again.

"Niewerland," Jan said.

Sparks said, "Ah," and looked at them thoughtfully. Then he said, "Do as you please," and started biting his nails again. "All right," said the cook, "I'll leave them to you," and he left.

"Message to all vessels heading for Zurland Estuary," the radio intoned. "Message for all vessels heading for Zurland Estuary. You will anchor between H.M.S. *Texel* and H.M.S *Ameland*, both of whom will direct their searchlights perpendicularly, and you'll wait for orders which will be conveyed to you by loud-hailer. I repeat . . ."

Sister came back, flushed and energetic, smelling of Lysol. "What's this?" she asked, seeing Adinda. "Not in bed yet?"

"She wasn't sleepy," Sparks said, "so the only course open to me was force, which I abhor."

"All right," said Sister, "it's just as well." She pulled back the bedclothes, lifted Jan out of the bunk, stooped and took Adinda by the hand. "Come on, children," she said. "I've got a nice quiet bed for you at the far end of the hospital, just next to my table. Come along."

"Have they called for it?" Sparks asked.

The sister said, "Yes," and took them away.

The long, low hospital smelled of Lysol and freshly planed wood. It was dimly lit by a blue lamp in the far corner; underneath the blue lamp stood a little table, with a wash basin and a pack of cotton wool on it. It was standing in front of an open fireplace framed in blue Delft tiles. Every bunk was occupied; next to the fireplace was a glass door leading to a corridor on a lower level, from which came the shrill persistent crying of a baby.

"All right, children," the sister said when they arrived at the table, and she pointed at the empty bunk next to it. "Here's your bed, nice and quiet. You're lucky to have it. Come on, Lucinda, undress, my dear." Adinda shook her head and sat down on the bunk, her head bent. The sister drew in her breath. "Now you don't want me to get angry with you, do you?" she asked, with forced kindliness. "Come, don't be silly. Undress, and when you're in bed I'll read a chapter of this lovely book to you. Now, are you going to undress, or aren't you?"

Adinda said nothing, but her shoulders started heaving. "Now listen, my good child," the sister said with an edge to her voice, "I won't stand for any nonsense. . . ."

A voice from the darkness called, feebly, "Sister . . . Sister . . ." Sister turned round and went along the passage between the bunks, her skirt rustling. She bent down over one of the still forms, and asked, "What's the matter, boy?"

"I think I'm bleeding," the feeble voice said, frightened.

"Well, it doesn't matter if you are," Sister answered gently, with a reassuring cheerfulness. "That's what I'm here for. Let me see." There was a short silence, then she said, "So you are, you naughty thing. Just a minute, we'll clear that up in a jiffy." She rustled back to the door beside the fireplace and called into the corridor, "Miss Winter! Miss—Winter!" her voice still hushed, but not tender any more. There was another rustle of skirts and a dim shape appeared in the doorway. "Yes, Sister?" the shape asked.

"Put those children to bed," the sister said. "I have to change a bandage."

"Where, Sister?" the shape asked.

"In Number One, where the meningitis was. Hurry up."

Skirts rustled as the sister walked briskly back between the bunks, and the vague shape came toward the children. She was a dark-haired girl, much younger than the sister, looking very tired. "Hallo," she said, with a catch in her throat. "I'm Miss Winter. Who are you?"

"I'm Jan Brink," Jan said brightly.

"Ssh!" said the girl. "Everybody is asleep. You must whisper. Hallo, Jan," and she held out her hand, which he took with suspicion. Then she bent over Adinda. "And who are you?" she whispered.

Adinda looked up; her face was expressionless, but tears glistened on her cheeks. "My goodness," the girl whispered, with exaggerated surprise. "I thought you were an old lady. Are you an old lady?"

Adinda shook her head.

"Well then, how old are you?" the girl whispered, her eyes wide.

Jan said, "Eleven. She's called Adinda, and her mother was a Negro."

Adinda turned on him and said, "Lll! Your mother is dead!"

"Pooh!" Jan said. "So's yours, and your father too, and your brothers, and your sisters. . . ."

"Children, children," the girl whispered. "You aren't going to fight, are you? If you do, Sister will be very angry with me."

Adinda got up and started unbuttoning her cardigan. Jan said, "I like Sister. She has adventures in a haystack."

"She what?" the girl asked, helping Adinda to take off her jewelry.

"A haystack," Jim said. "She gave Sparks her members."

"I beg your pardon?" asked the girl, who had knelt down in front of Adinda, and she looked up at him, forgetting what she was doing.

"Members. . . ." Jan repeated, waveringly. "Memories. . . ."

The girl looked at Adinda, her face blank, and suddenly she was overcome by helpless giggles. She put her arms round Adinda and hid her face in the cardigan.

While Jan stood looking at them, offended, Sister came striding briskly from the darkness, carrying a basin with stained cotton wool. The stains were green in the blue light. "What's this?" she asked. "Miss Winter, what are you doing?"

Adinda said, "She's undressing me."

Sister snapped, in a whisper, "Well, get a move on! You're blocking the passage." Then she rustled off into the dim corridor.

When she was gone, the girl showed her face, wiped her eyes with the back of her hand and said, "Thank you, Adinda. Let's go to bed."

Adinda eyed her coldly, said, "All right," and took off her bonnet.

In one of the bunks in the darkness, someone started moaning. The girl, still on her knees, looked anxiously over her shoulder.

"Go ahead," Adinda said. "I can undress myself."

The girl got to her feet and tiptoed away between the bunks. When the sister came back with the empty basin, Adinda was lying in bed, her clothes neatly folded on the blankets, and Jan was sitting on the edge of the bunk, his hands in his lap, pouting.

"What's the matter, little boy?" Sister asked. "Where's Miss Winter?"

Jan said, gloomily, "She's left us," and the sister drew in her breath again. She rustled away into the darkness, and there was a sound of hissing whispers. Then Adinda softly put out a small brown hand, felt caressingly for the tenderest part of his buttock, and pinched it like the bite of a snake. Jan screamed "Ouch!" and jumped; the two women came rushing toward them from the blue darkness. "Darling! What's the matter?" Sister asked, with concern.

Jan stuck out his lower lip, sniffed and whispered, "She pinched me."

"Did she now?" the sister asked. Then she turned on Adinda and said, "Will you please make room for him, young woman, or must I put you with the cook?"

Adinda gave her a motionless black stare, that lasted until a fraction of a second before Sister's hand flew up to hit her. Then she moved aside without a word.

"All right, dear," the sister said to Jan, patting him on the back. "In you go. And now don't let me hear a squeak out of either of you again tonight. Miss Winter will read to you for a few minutes, and then you'll go to sleep as good as gold, and I'll wake you up with a cup of tea in the morning."

After she had rustled off once more and vanished through the door next to the fireplace, the girl whispered, "Do you want me to read about the haystack? Or do you want me to tell you a story?"

Neither of them answered.

"Perhaps you'd like to tell me a story yourself?" the girl whispered, her head close to them.

"Do you know what a cremated is?" Jan asked.

Adinda snorted.

Jan hissed, "Piss off, you little bloodsucker, or I'll smash you!"

The girl gasped in the darkness, and Adinda snorted again.

The girl rubbed her eyes, and there was a short silence. Then she whispered, "Look, children. It's very late, and we're all very tired, and you mustn't make Sister angry, for she's a wonderful woman who has worked like ten horses, and if she ticks me off again, I'll burst into tears. So let me tell you a story, or you tell me a story, or anything you like, as long as you keep quiet, and go to sleep."

"Haven't you got a mouth organ?" Jan asked.

The girl sighed, "No."

Then Adinda said, "Before I went to sleep, I used to listen to the gamelang, and then, when I was almost asleep, he would play his flute."

Jan asked, "Who would?"

"The shepherd," Adinda answered, softly. "He would play every night, and I tried to stay awake to listen. I tried to frighten myself to stay awake, by thinking of hantus and snakes. Fat black snakes, sneaking down the poles of the veranda. But he would play, and play, and I would get so sleepy that I thought of the sea, and the big waves breaking on the beach. They were like green fires in the dark."

"Fires," Jan said, contemptuously. "How can waves be fires?"

"They were," Adinda whispered. "They would rise far away, and come silently toward us, and then they would turn into green fire down from the top, and then they would stretch out on the beach, and hiss, and go dark again."

Jan mumbled, sleepily, "Pooh. Fire."

Adinda went on, "I sat there secretly, with Kromo. When it was too hot to sleep we tiptoed out, afraid of snakes and kalongs, but we would always get there in the end, and sit down, and listen to the waves, and look. . . ."

Then she fell silent, and listened to the soft breathing of Miss Winter.

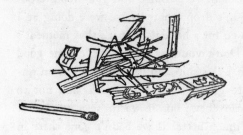

Jan woke up in the middle of the night. The blue light was still burning, but the sister, whom he had seen sitting reading at her table every time he had opened his eyes, was gone. He sat up, leaned out and looked down the dark passage between the bunks. At the far end, on the left, where the steps were that led down to the dining room, he saw lights and heard voices. He got up and tiptoed down the passage.

The dim shapes in the bunks were all lying motionless. On the steps two men were sitting with their backs to him. As he stealthily crept up behind them and peered over their shoulders, he saw, seated on the bench round the dining room table, the cook, the wireless operator, a fat man, the sister and Miss Winter. At the head of the table sat a man in a duffel coat, with gray hair and blue eyes, whom he recognized from the photograph of the houseboat's interior that hung on the wall. The man looked thin and tired, and there was something sad about him. He sat splintering a matchbox nervously while he talked.

"I know, I know," he said. "Of course not. It's preposterous even to say that. We didn't drop whatever we were doing at a moment's notice, just to go for a holiday. But it's that moment's notice that worries me. Don't you see? So far we've done good work, despite the fact that this ship and its crew are just an improvisation. I want us to go on doing good work, and not to bite off more than we can chew. For if we make a mess of it over there, it would be much better if we hadn't gone there in the first place."

"I think that maybe you are just very tired, Mr. Tadema," a quiet voice said. It was the doctor's. Jan couldn't see him, for he was sitting in the corner next to the stairs. "It's good to be aware of our limitations, but we mustn't go too far and underestimate ourselves. If we happen to be the only hospital ship that can get in, we just have to go there and make the best of it. Don't you agree, Smithy?"

"I do," the fat man said. "I've come here to help, and I'm quite ready to meet anything that comes my way."

"Well, I don't know," one of the men in front of Jan said. "I'd like to hear some more before I make up my mind. Of course, I'm ready to help, like all of us. I didn't leave my nursery with three acres of young plants under glass in the hands of my wife and a youngster, to come and twiddle my thumbs over here. But I don't want to come home with typhoid fever, particularly as I gather that it's mainly the Army and the Navy who are left there. Well, I came to help the civilians. The Army and the Navy can look after themselves. That's what I'm paying income tax for."

"I don't quite agree with that, I think," the gray-haired man said carefully, making a tidy little heap of the splinters of his matchbox. "The organization is bad, we all know that, but then it's bound to be, because I assure you that neither of us has a really complete idea of the vastness of the disaster. If there are a hundred young boys living in nightmarish circumstances, without water, lights, warmth, without a change of clothes. . . ."

"Come, come," the nurseryman said. "Surely they've got warm clothes, blankets, camp beds. . . ."

"They haven't," said the gray-haired man. "They rushed off on Saturday night in their small open boats, taking nothing with them but what they could lay hands on. Not one of them has a blanket. They sleep on the bare benches in the ruin of a church, with empty sandbags for blankets. They haven't got any clothes apart from the pair of blue overalls they hastily put on before leaving. In those, they handle the corpses, eat and sleep; most of them haven't even got rubber boots. The Air Force dropped three hundred pairs of hip boots yesterday, but they were all size five."

"What?" Sparks asked.

"Size five," the gray-haired man said, wearily. "The only one who could wear them was the local doctor's wife. And it isn't only the sailors and the soldiers that need us. There are about a hundred civilians left, and every single one of them, in my opinion, is crazy. I know this sounds an exaggeration, but I swear to you it is true. There they are, in that horrible village of ruins, with three hundred corpses still lying under the wreckage, surrounded by a floating desert of filth, in which there are at least three thousand dead cattle. The stench in that village has to be smelled to be believed. Well, there they are, in this indescribable mess, and they walk about grinning, doing absolutely nothing, saying that if only all these foreigners would leave, they would clear up the village in a couple of days. Well, good God, I know I'm not an expert, but any sane man can see that the only thing to do with that village and the desert of destruction that surrounds it is to take out every living soul, put a sanitary cordon around it, wait till the water goes down and then burn it with bombs and flamethrowers. I've never seen anything so ghastly, nor so desperately hopeless in all my life. It's worse than anything I saw during the war, a hundred times worse. It is, well . . . I suppose it's just unimaginable."

"What exactly do you want us to do then?" the other man in front of Jan asked. He had a quiet, kind voice and white hair. He smelled of mothballs. The smell came from the yachtsman's pullover he was wearing.

"Thank you, judge," said the nurseryman. "I was about to put the same question. Apart from giving baths to the boys who handle the corpses, and looking after small casualties that may occur, what can we do, considering that there is hardly anyone left? Here the ill and the wounded pour in by the dozen. It seems a pity to leave the work that we're doing, unless there's something better for us to do."

"Well," said the gray-haired man. "That is what I've been thinking about during all those hours the Y-boat was aground. When we first entered the village, and I didn't yet realize how bad it was, I'm afraid I made a rather rash promise to the local doctor and some civilians, to whom I described our ship. They were so delighted at the idea that we might be coming that I promised we would. One of the civilians offered his services as a pilot, for the harbor is very difficult to get into, and all the buoys are washed away. I said: all right, the Y-boat is going back to Bruinisse in about three hours' time, be here and we'll take you back with us, so tomorrow you can pilot the hospital ship in. Then I started wandering about the village. I helped the doctor, with some Marines, to push his car to a garage. It had been submerged and was full of mud, and its wheels squeaked horribly as we pushed it. The doctor was very grateful and said, 'Splendid. Now they can start fixing it up at once.' I looked inside the garage and it was full of corpses."

"You mean, of people that were drowned there?" the fat man they had called Smithy asked.

"No," said the gray-haired man. "The garage, so I found out later, is one of the morgues. The one for men. There's another one for women, and one for children. The Navy collects them from the houses and the wreckage with their rowing boats, the Army identifies them with a committee of civilians, and the Marines put them in their coffins and bury them."

"Where?" asked Sparks.

"In a hole in the dike near the harbor. They go in ten at a time and are given a communal service. There are two wonderful old men there, a Protestant clergyman and a Catholic priest, both looking like tramps. Those two also go to the outlying farms with the Navy, to convince the farmers and their families who are still sitting in their haylofts that they must leave."

"Do you mean to say that there are still people in the polder?" the judge asked.

The gray-haired man nodded. "Hundreds of them," he answered. "They refuse to leave. Some of them say that they'll wait until the water goes down, and that they won't leave their houses to be pilfered. But most of them refuse to leave because they think the floods are a punishment of God for their sins, and they should not defy Him any further. As I told you, in my opinion, everybody still alive in and around that village is raving mad. Take the doctor's wife, for instance. She said to me, 'Ah, lovely. Tomorrow or the day after, when you're all gone, I'll give my house a good spring-cleaning.' I still thought there wasn't much wrong with that, until I saw her house. Only half of it is left standing. You can see into all the rooms."

"That still doesn't answer our question what we are supposed to do," the nurseryman said.

"Well, goodness," Sister said briskly. "Nurse them, of course! You can't leave those people to themselves. If all we could do is just make them cups of tea, and let them sit here in this very dining room, nice and cozy, and laugh and smoke cigarettes, I think we would already be doing a wonderful job."

"That's exactly my own line of thought," the gray-haired man said. "At least, it was in the beginning. I thought: here we are with this ship, I know it's a hospital now, but it still has a homelike atmosphere with its lights and its central heating. I thought: what a wonderful thing it would be to people who have survived a disaster, and who've been living in a nightmare ever since, just to take a bath and put on clean clothes and drink a glass of geneva, and talk about normal things for once, instead of only about who's been found and who is still missing, or about old farmer So-and-so, whom you can still see lying in his bed from the crown of the dike, over the wreck of his stable, in which there are sixty-nine head of cattle lying dead in their ropes, side by side, three rows of them."

"In his bed?" the judge asked. "Why haven't they taken him out?"

"They can't," said the gray-haired man. "Between the dike and the house is the water, covered with floating wreckage. You can't walk on that, and what's more: if you as much as touch those houses, they collapse. Twice during the three hours I was there, I heard a rumble in the distance. The second time I saw by chance what it was: a house, far away, collapsing."

"Well," said the doctor, "I know you must be full of what you saw, and don't think I'm not interested or touched by it, but I would like to know what made you change your mind. Why are you asking us whether we should go or not?"

The gray-haired man sighed, and rubbed his face. "Perhaps it is just that I am scared stiff," he said finally, "but my main reason is that I don't think we can cope with it. What these people need is the care of professional psychiatrists, not just a handful of well-meaning individuals, who left their jobs and their houses on the spur of the moment, and who've got nothing to offer but a drink and their sympathy. I'm afraid they are too far gone just to relax in congenial surroundings, and then go back to that nightmare. I think they'll hate the sight of us, for if we haven't got a clear-cut job to do in that horrible village, we'll just be sightseers. Not that there are any; the village is banned to anyone without a pass from the military commander, and the only contact is by helicopter. It's the most thoroughly isolated place in the area."

The doctor's white-sleeved arm held out a pack of cigarettes to him; he took one, put it in his mouth, and forgot it. "Well," he said, "that's about it, friends. I could sit here for hours, talking about what I've seen, but I don't suppose it would make the picture any clearer. I think the frankest way I can put it is this: in my heart of hearts, I know we should go there; but I hope to find a very good reason why we can't. When the Y-boat left, the pilot came running. The sailors on board didn't see him, but I did. Yet I behaved as if I didn't. The engines made a lot of noise so they didn't hear him calling; but I did. We got out of the harbor, nosed our way down the channel, and ran aground about a mile away. While we lay there, waiting for the tide to come up, I saw a little black figure wading toward us from the broken dike. He waded all the way out to us, until he came within hailing distance. The water was up to his waist then. It was the pilot. I shouted to him through the megaphone, saying that in the meantime we had heard on the radio that all evacuation ships were to concentrate on Dreischor Estuary so I didn't know whether we would come tomorrow. He said he understood, but he'd be waiting for us on the dike at high tide and row out." There was a silence, in which he lit his cigarette. "When I think of that pilot," he said, "I feel . . . well, I feel ashamed, I suppose. But so far, frankly, my fear is stronger."

"What if you went to bed, Tadema?" the judge said. "We've all had a few hours' rest. You've been up and about since dawn. Go to sleep and let us talk it over among ourselves. I suppose that whatever we decide, you'll agree with."

"Yes."

"Well, all right, leave it to us then. But there is one thing I should like to know before you go away. Is it your ship you are worrying about? After all, it's your house. Your family lives on it. Are you sure that you're not afraid of contaminating it, or ruining it? For, in that case, we'll all understand."

The nurseryman said, "Hear, hear."

The gray-haired man shrugged his shoulders. "Good God, no," he said. "I came here ready to lose it. One can't go halfway with this kind of thing. If I lose my house, well—I'll still have my wife and children, and that's more than many others can say just now."

He got up. He was much smaller than Jan had expected.

[124]

"All right," he said. "I suppose you'll come in and tell me when you've made up your minds. I'll lie down for a while."

After he was gone, the others were silent; then the fat Smithy said, "I hope I'll have that valve fixed tonight, for we can't sail without it."

Then the gray-haired man came back, angry. "What the hell is this?" he asked. "My bunk is full of animals!"

"Oh," said Sister, "I'm so sorry. They came with two stray children the Urkers brought in this evening. I'd forgotten all about them."

"Yes," said the doctor, "that reminds me: what are we supposed to do with our patients? We can't take them with us to Onderkerk."

"So you have decided?" the gray-haired man said. "That's quick work, I must say."

There was an embarrassed silence.

"Such dear little children," the sister said. "One of them is a little half-caste."

"All right," said the gray-haired man. "If I've made the prospect attractive enough for you to make up your minds without discussion, I suppose it's my own fault."

"Go to bed, Tadema," the judge said. "We'll talk about it, I promise you."

The gray-haired man turned round, and he had almost vanished in the corridor to the aft-cabin when he suddenly stopped and asked, "Half-caste, did you say?"

The sister said, "Yes. What's the matter?"

"What age?"

"Oh, about twelve, I should say."

"A girl?"

"Yes."

"With a little boy aged ten, fair hair, blue eyes, called Jan?"

"Yes. Why? Do you know about them?"

"Yes," said the gray-haired man. "The old clergyman in Onderkerk asked whether I had seen them. They were lost in Niewerland, where he came from. They are his adopted children."

"Well," said the doctor. "Two patients less to worry about."

"No question of it!" the gray-haired man said, sharply. "If you are considering for one second taking children to Onderkerk, you can't have understood what I've been trying to explain to you all along! I'm willing to go there, if you decide on it, but now you suggest this, I must warn you that you don't know what you are deciding. Those children are out of the question."

"But my dear Tadema . . ." the doctor began.

"No question of it!" the gray-haired man said. "I'd sooner take two children to Devil's Island."

"But their father is there!" Sister said cheerfully. "Surely you're not going to send those children on to the reception center, to have them farmed out with some totally strange family inland, if their father is just a couple of miles away, and we are actually going there?"

"I don't care if their whole family is there!" the gray-haired man said. "I will not take any children to Onderkerk, and that's final. The local doctor sent his two children away as well, and those that are left will be taken out at any moment."

"Are there still children there?" Miss Winter asked, timidly.

The gray-haired man said, "Yes, and I hope I'll never set eyes on them again." He turned to go. "And for your sakes, I hope that they'll be gone when you arrive," he added. Then he walked away.

Jan crept stealthily back to his bunk. Adinda was still asleep, one arm outstretched, her mouth open, ghostly in the blue light. When he slipped under the blankets, she stirred and mumbled, "Where are we going now?"

"To Onderkerk," Jan said.

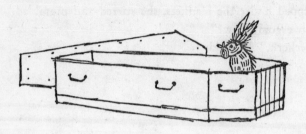

The children were woken up early by Sister shaking them by the shoulder and calling, "Up you get, children! Dress quickly! Breakfast is ready!"

All the patients were awake; the hospital was noisy, and very smelly. Miss Winter, pale and flustered, rustled up and down with bedpans; from every bunk someone was calling her. An old woman wailed, "Sister, Sister . . ."; an old man with a stubbly gray chin sat upright in a dirty Jaeger vest with short sleeves, crying, "Hey woman, the bottle! I'm not a camel!" There was only one bunk in which the patient lay still; the doctor and the sister stood bent over it.

Jan could not wake up. Adinda shook him, cried, "Jan! Jan!" He said, "Coming," but he said it in his sleep. He had been lying awake most of the night, thinking about Mr. Grijpma, and how they could get to Onderkerk. When finally Adinda's persistent shaking dragged him to the surface from a blue darkness full of waving seaweed, he clutched her wrists and whispered, "Adinda! I've got something to tell you!"

Adinda said, "Get up." She was half-dressed already.

"It's very important!" Jan whispered. "We must hide, we must fetch the animals and look for a hiding place. Quick!"

"A hiding place?"

"Here," he said, "here, on board this ship! It's going to Onderkerk this morning, and Mr. Tadema doesn't want to take any children with him, and the animals are asleep in his bunk, and . . ."

"Come on, everybody, get a move on!" the sister called, rustling past. "Get dressed by yourself if you can, and if you can't, lie perfectly still until somebody comes to help you. You are going to be transferred to another ship."

Jan whispered, "You hear?" and all the patients started asking questions. In the midst of the hubbub, Adinda dressed methodically. She spread a handkerchief on the blankets, put her jewelry inside and knotted it into a small bag. Jan pulled his clothes on, untidily; when he took her by the hand to take her outside, she asked, "Have you got everything?"

"Of course, of course," Jan whispered. "Come on."

"You haven't," she said. "There's your penknife, and you haven't got your hat. Where are your socks?"

Jan stamped his foot with impatience. "Come on," he said. Haven't you heard what I said? If we don't hide at once, they'll take us away and we'll never get to Onderkerk."

"Put your socks on," Adinda said. "If you don't take all your belongings with you, they'll be gone when you come back. I know."

Jan stuffed his penknife into the pocket of his apron, put on his socks and took her hand again to lead her outside.

"Your hat," she said. "Do you want it? If you don't take it with you now, it will be stolen."

Jan slammed the toque with the osprey feathers on his head; then, at last, she yielded and he took her to the steps that led to the deck.

"Children, where are you going?" Sister's voice called out behind them. "Breakfast is in the dining room!"

"We want to go out for . . . for a breather," Jan said lamely.

"Go to the dining room!" the sister commanded. "No nonsense."

They moved reluctantly toward the dining room, then a patient called, "Sister, I've finished!" As she turned away, Jan pulled Adinda up the steps to the deck. She stumbled and fell on her knees, but she didn't cry out.

The deck was cold and windy, the day wild and gray. The air was rent by explosions from the exhausts of fishing smacks leaving the harbor; a blue motorboat barked orders at them through its loud-hailer. A helicopter hovered in the sky, descending; the drone of the engine grew to a roar. Jan took Adinda into a corner beside the big steering wheel of the barge and whispered, "Listen, quick, before anyone comes. . . . This ship is going to Onderkerk, and they want to take us off, but we must stay on board, for Father is there."

Adinda looked at him with a flash of hope. "Where?" she asked.

"In Onderkerk."

Then her face fell, and she looked at him with suspicion. "How do you know that?"

"I got out of bed last night," Jan whispered, "and I overheard them talking. Father is in Onderkerk, digging graves and talking to farmers, in a little boat."

"Don't lie," she said, sullenly.

"I swear to you it's true," Jan whispered. "He asked Mr. Tadema if he had any news about a half-caste girl aged eleven, and a fair-haired boy called Jan, and he said we were his adopted children."

"How could he be in Onderkerk?" she asked, "when Mother is in the tower?"

"He must have floated," Jan said, "just like we did. Perhaps he was just closing the flap of the henhouse, after Mother took Prince out. And then, when the water came, he climbed on top of it and floated to Onderkerk. Don't you remember? The place where Mrs. Ool's houseboat ran aground? Those sailors said they were going to tow us to a little village that was all broken, and that was just round the corner, and then the rope broke and the Urkers picked us up; well, that was Onderkerk. Perhaps he has floated behind us all the time, trying to catch up with us."

Adinda looked at the harbor, the gray warships, the crown of the dike, along which a herd of tired and muddy cattle was driven by soldiers. "He isn't in Onderkerk," she said. "He is dead, and we'll never see him again. They'll send us to another ship, and then yet another, and then to an orphanage, and there we'll stay until the next thing happens."

"All right," said Jan. "If you want to be silly, go to an orphanage. I'll go to Onderkerk, and I'll take Bussy with me."

"I'd much rather go to an orphanage this time," Adinda said. "I don't want any more fathers and mothers."

"That's a nice thing to say!" Jan said. "I like them."

Adinda shrugged her shoulders and said, "So did I."

"All right," said Jan, "good-by," and he got to his feet.

She looked up at him, her eyes calm and sad. "Good-by," she said.

Jan hesitated, then he sat down again, grumbling.

They sat looking at the blue motorboat, alongside a cluster of fishing smacks. "*UK 19!*" the loud-hailer barked. "Stop talking to your neighbor and get a move on! You're blocking the fairway! . . . *UK 19!*" The helicopter had landed in a shunting yard at the foot of the dike, between two upturned goods wagons that lay across the rails. A van with a red cross wobbled toward it; its back doors opened and sailors with empty stretchers jumped out. Then a hatch in the deck in front of the steering wheel was slowly opened, and Sparks' head appeared, his hair tousled, his eyes light with sleep. "Hullo there," he said, when he saw the children.

They stared at him gloomily.

"What's the matter?"

"She won't believe that this ship is going to Onderkerk," Jan said. "She won't believe that Father is there."

Sparks said, "Ah."

"You tell her it's true, mister," Jan said. "You were there when he told them. You tell her, she won't believe me."

"How do you know all this?" Sparks asked. "You were supposed to be in bed, sleeping the sleep of the innocent."

"I wasn't," said Jan. "I was sitting behind the nurseryman, and I heard everything."

A plane roared overhead, very low. Sparks looked up at it, then he came out. He closed the hatch gingerly. As he stood in the wind, his jacket and his trousers jellying, he stretched and yawned, and said, "Another gale warning over the wireless, as if we didn't know."

"Tell her, mister," Jan urged him. "Isn't it true? Isn't Father in Onderkerk and isn't the ship going there today?"

Sparks stared at him; then he said, casually, "I suppose that's fair enough."

Jan's eyes filled with tears and his lip trembled as he said, "Why don't you tell her? You were there, I saw you."

Sparks sighed; then he squatted in front of them and put his hands on their knees. "Listen," he said. "You'd better forget that, because whatever you do, they won't take you to Onderkerk."

"But Father is there, isn't he?" Jan asked. "Tell her he is there, please."

Sparks looked at Adinda, her masklike face, her sad eyes. Then he said, "That's right."

"Ah," said Jan, "you see? That'll teach you to call me a liar, you bloodsucker."

"Hey, hey!" said Sparks. "That's not the spirit at all. Now listen, and try to be as grown-up as you can. . . ."

"I'll ask Mr. Tadema myself," Jan said. "We'll go and see him together."

Sparks shook his head. "Listen," he said. "If this were my ship, I would take you. As it happens, I am the only professional sailor on board; the rest of the crew consists of well-intentioned gentlemen who have never sailed outside the Loosdrecht lakes. You can't expect an architect, a market gardener, a blacksmith, a Sunday-school teacher and a judge to take two children across the open sea, in a river barge, in a gale, to a place which they consider is worse than hell."

"The doctor would take us," Jan said, defiantly. "So would Sister, so would you. Can't you hide us somewhere? Can't you put us underneath your desk, or behind the little door where the central heating is?"

Sparks shook his head and said, "Listen. . . ."

"I'm sure the doctor could hide us somewhere," Jan said; "surely the sister and he have got a cabin?"

[133]

Sparks rubbed his nose. The helicopter took off again, roaring, and the ambulance wobbled away, its doors shut. A hooter boomed outside the harbor, and a big white ship with the letters "O.M." on its bow slowly nosed its way in among the scurrying fishing smacks.

"There's the *Van der Steng*," Sparks said. "She's going to take you on board with the patients. You'll like it, she's a lovely ship. She'll take you to Rotterdam, to the Ahoy Hall, where there must be thousands of people by now, waiting to be farmed —to be sent inland. In a week's time your father will be with you, somewhere nice and dry and cozy."

"We don't want to go to Rotterdam," Jan said. "We want to go to Father now. Don't we, Adinda?"

Adinda looked at Sparks with her sad eyes and said calmly, "Yes."

"Well," said Sparks, "just as you like. But don't expect this ship to take you there. Quite frankly, I think you're lucky not to be sailing with us, for the trip is sure to be a nightmare, with everybody running about, shouting, spearing each other with punting poles, and the women being seasick. Why don't you go for a walk along the quay and see if there isn't a proper ship with professional sailors going to Onderkerk? Ask the fishermen. They won't mind taking you on if they hear your father is there."

"Will you come with us?" Jan asked. "Please, mister, come with us. They won't listen to just children."

Sparks shook his head. "No, my friend," he said. "If you want to go to Onderkerk that much, go and fend for yourself. Come, get a move on. As soon as the *Van der Steng* has berthed, they'll come for the patients. If you want to sail to Onderkerk, you'll have to be out of sight when they start looking for you."

"But our animals!" Jan said. "We can't go without the animals. Where are they?"

"I slept with about a dozen," Sparks said, "all hair and claws. I wouldn't be up here at this ungodly hour if one of them hadn't started licking my nose."

"That's Bussy," Jan said. "Have you got the cat and the rabbit too?"

"Are you sure that was all?" Sparks asked. Then he relented and said, "All right, wait here."

He opened the hatch again and climbed backward down the ladder. The white ship boomed; the little blue motorboat came speeding toward it, quacking. "We'll try to find an Urker," Jan said. "Perhaps the *UK 516* is there, or Meter. They'll certainly take us to Onderkerk if we ask them, they're our friends."

Adinda stared at the white ship, and shrugged her shoulders.

Sparks came back, his arms full of radiant animals. Bussy yapped as he saw them, and started to wriggle. "Easy, easy," Sparks said, putting them down on the deck. "Little Buzzard needn't relieve himself for some time, he's done it in the captain's boots." As Adinda picked up Noisette and stooped to pick up Ko, he added, "I think you'd better attach those animals to a string or something, for if they get away from you they'll be shot."

"Shot?" Jan asked, horrified. "Who'll shoot them?"

"The Military Police," Sparks answered. "All stray animals in the flooded area are shot at sight. They say it's against contamination from the corpses."

"We haven't got any leads," Jan said. "Could you let us have some string, mister?"

Sparks scratched his head, then he fingered the end of a rope that was looped up on deck, around a set of pulleys. "Have you got a knife on you?" he asked. Jan handed him his penknife, and he looked round. "Well," he said, as he snapped the knife open, "if any of these stage-sailors sees me do this I'll probably be keel-hauled. If they don't, they'll never notice." He cut off a length of rope as long as his arm. "Use the strands," he said, handing it to Jan. "There are three of them."

Jan started to unravel the rope but Sparks took him by the arm. "Do that ashore, my friend," he said, "and do it out of sight. Well, good-by and good luck."

He gently pushed them down the steep gangway, Jan carrying Bussy, Adinda with Ko and Noisette. They squatted behind a stack of barrels and made leads for the animals out of the rope; then they set out along the mudtrack that had once been a paved road, skirting the harbor.

The animals could not walk in the mud; they had to carry them. Their feet seemed to sink deeper into the mire at every step. A siren howled behind them, they jumped aside, and while Adinda cried, "My clog! My clog!" a boat on wheels lurched past them, splashing them with mud from head to foot. Noisette struggled to get free; Adinda, standing on one leg, had to drop her. After Jan had dug out the clog, she took Noisette in her arms once more; the kitten looked like a muddy rat. They plodded past a row of newly dug graves with unplaned crosses on the edge of the shunting yard, and toiled on to where the fishing smacks lay. Another helicopter roared down, another ambulance came splashing and swaying toward them, honking its horn. The fishing smacks were lying far out, against the mooring poles, and there was no gangplank to connect them with the shore. Jan shouted at the fishermen that stood talking on the foredeck of the first smack: "Urker! Hey, Urker!" then the blue boat, hidden behind the ships, barked, *"Elburg 17! El-*

burg 17! Moor alongside the hospital ship over starboard!" As the men did not hear Jan's feeble shout, he and Adinda cried together, "Urker! Urker!" but they couldn't put their hands to their mouths because of the animals, and the wind swept their shouts away. They stumbled on, bewildered and lost, frightened by the noise and the devastation around them.

At the far end of the harbor they scrambled up the dike, slithering. When they got to the crown, they saw that the port was just a lonely basin full of ships in a wilderness of water; the sea was on all sides. To the right, far away, was a half-submerged village. The wind and the water had washed a wide belt of wreckage up against the dike: planks, bits of beds, shutters, swollen dead animals, a perambulator, a pillow with the word "Help" painted on it. Above the waterline, a muddy footpath had been trodden into the dike; soldiers, sailors and fishermen were slogging along it toward the village in the distance. A boy with a fur cap and in long baggy trousers came squelching toward them, leaning against the wind. Jan called, "Urker!" plaintively. The boy stood still and asked, "What the hell do you mean, 'Urker,' you Protestant midget? Can't you see I'm from Volendam?"

Jan stammered, "Sorry, sir. I wondered whether you were going to Onderkerk. Our father . . ."

"Even if I was going there, I wouldn't take you," the boy said, "after calling my mother a bitch and my father a bandit. Urk!" He said the word with venom, and spat. A growling voice behind the children asked, "What was that you said, you handful of snot?" The boy stared, and the children cowered. Two huge Urkers were standing behind them.

"Excuse me, Urker," Jan said, with desperate courage; but the Urkers did not listen to him. One of them put out a paw toward the Volendammer boy, who screamed, "Help! Skipper! Help!" and started to run back toward an approaching group of fishermen; the Urker flung a fistful of mud after him. The fishermen talked to the boy; then they came swaggering toward the Urkers. The Urkers went to meet them; they talked; and suddenly one of them, in long baggy trousers, flew bodily through the air, hit the driftwood, toppled over and crashed into the perambulator. There were screams and shouts, a whistle throbbed, soldiers with white helmets slid down the dike brandishing white truncheons; Jan dragged Adinda back onto the crown of the dike, but there a file of horses came lumbering toward them, gray with mud up to their haunches, their eyes shut, like sleepwalkers. A voice called, "Watch out, children!" and arms pulled them back from behind. As the horses rumbled past, the voice said, "I don't understand why they don't shoot them on the spot. They won't live." Then someone turned Jan's head round and he saw two soldiers in battle dress, unshaven, dirty. "What are you wandering about for?" one of the soldiers asked.

"We're looking for a ship to take us to Onderkerk," Jan said, his lip trembling. "Our father is there."

"Go to the hospital ship *Honesta*," the soldier said. "Over there, in the far corner. They're leaving for Onderkerk."

Jan said miserably, "Thank you." He took Adinda by the arm, carrying Bussy in the other, and they squelched away. Jan started to cry. "Wait!" a voice called after them. It was one of the soldiers. "That cart will take you there! He's going that way!" He pointed at a cart loaded with coffins, pulled by a white pony that looked as if it were wearing muddy hip boots. He stopped it, talked to the driver, then he beckoned the children. "Hop on," he said, as they came struggling back. "They'll give you some clothes there too. Where did you get the ones you're wearing?"

Jan stammered, "They—they were given to us."

"No kidding," the soldier said. His companion grinned and said, "Someone had a grim sense of humor, or maybe they came out of a Red Cross parcel from Tibet."

"Well, up you go," the first soldier said, lifting Jan and Bussy. He put them on top of a coffin. Then he lifted Ko and Noisette, then Adinda. "Look after yourselves!" he called as the cart started wobbling away. "Don't fall off!" At the bottom of the dike, about a dozen fishermen were now fighting.

As they sat on the swaying coffin, holding on with both hands, they felt sick and cold, and Jan started to cry again. Adinda put her hand over his and so they drove on, back to where they had come from.

As they drew near, they saw that a fishing smack had moored alongside the hospital ship and was taking over stretchers with patients. No one noticed the cart; everyone on deck was busy with the patients.

The driver and a passing sailor helped them down. Then the two men unloaded the coffins, and put them behind the barrels on the quayside. "Good-by, children," the driver said. "Don't hang around here, or you'll catch cold." Then he turned the cart, jumped onto the seat, lashed the pony with the bridle, cried, "Hee!" and drove off, ploughing through the mud.

Jan started off toward the gangway, crestfallen; but Adinda held him back.

"What?" he asked.

She opened a coffin and put the animals in. "Give me your handkerchief," she said.

"What are you doing?"

"Give me your handkerchief. Quick!"

"I haven't got one."

She undid the knots of the handkerchief in which she had carried her jewelry. It was dirty now, for she had dropped it several times. She put the jewelry inside the coffin, and tied the handkerchief around Bussy's snout. Then she got in herself, and beckoned Jan. "Get in," she said. "Quick! Help me put back the lid before anyone sees us."

He obeyed. Together they lifted the lid and put it back over their heads. It became dark. The darkness smelled of wood shavings.

"It's very stuffy," Jan said.

Adinda said, "Ssh!"

They sat in the darkness, motionless, for a long time. It got hotter and hotter. They started sweating, the air became thick. Jan was about to lift the lid to let some fresh air in, when they heard sucking steps in the mud around them, and voices.

"Would you believe it?" someone said. "More coffins for Onderkerk. They must be crazy." It was Sparks.

"These are different," another voice said. "Most of them are for children. Come on, let's get them aboard. Tadema is worrying already because he thinks we'll miss the tide."

The steps squelched around them, then went away.

"I'm afraid," Jan said.

Adinda said, "Ssh!"

Bussy growled in the darkness, and he could be heard scratching.

The steps came back.

"Which one next?" asked a voice they did not recognize. They heard Sparks answer, "Let's take that big one first."

There was a loud squeak and a rumble, as the handles of their coffin were pulled up. Then it started to move. It swayed, it heaved, and thudded on the ground again.

"Christ!" said Sparks' voice. "They've sent us a full one!"

They were nearly suffocated, and it came as a relief when the lid was opened and cold air rushed in. They blinked in the blinding sunlight and vaguely saw two silhouettes bent over them, staring. Then they heard Sparks' voice say, "Fair enough," and the lid was shut again.

Someone whistled, and Sparks' voice hollered, "Smithy! Cook! Give us a hand with this coffin, boys. We can't manage."

The gangway squeaked in the distance as steps came rumbling down it. Then Cook's voice said, "Come, come! Can't you two big boys even lift an empty coffin? What will you do when it's full?"

"Very well," said Sparks. "You try. Come on."

Cook's voice said: "All right. Judge, Smithy, Tweedledum—when I say 'Heave,' heave. Heave!"

The coffin rose and thudded back.

Cook's voice said, "Phew! What's inside, stones?"

Someone whispered.

"Go on," Cook said. "Who put them in there? You?"

"No," said Sparks. "It's all their own work."

Cook said, "Well, I'll be . . ." and the lid of the coffin opened to a crack. Sparks' voice called, "Don't! Sister is looking for them all over the place; if we go on opening and shutting it we'll give them away. The point is, do we want to give them away?"

There was a silence, then the judge said, "Let's try again."

Cook called, "Ready? Heave!"

The coffin rose once more, and was carried on board, swaying and bumping. Noisette started to miaow; she only became silent when the coffin was put down again. Then there came a crack of light, and a draft of fresh air. Someone had put something under the lid, to keep it slightly open. Jan fingered the object gingerly, and discovered it was a pipe.

"Adinda!" he called, in a whisper. "Adinda, what . . ."

Adinda said, "Ssh!"

"I can't understand it," Jan whispered. "What are they doing?"

Adinda said, "Playing."

"At what?" he asked.

She said, "Ssh!" again, and he gave up.

They were taken out an hour
later, when the ship was at sea. They had listened, breathless,
to the shouts, the banging, the rattling, the squeaking of pulleys
and the cannonlike thunder of flapping sails; then the whole
ship started to move. It not only plunged and reared as the
Urker ship had done; it heeled over at so steep an angle that
Jan and Bussy slid down on top of Adinda, Ko and Noisette.
The wind whistled in the rigging, spray lashed their coffin like
hail, and every time the flat bow of the ship hit a wave, it shuddered and stopped as if it had run aground.

When they were let out by Sister, Sparks and the judge, they
were badly shaken. Sister was very angry, but more so with
Sparks and the judge than with them. As they were carried along
the heaving deck, they saw that the sails were hoisted. They were
big and brown, and veined with spray like huge dead leaves. At
the steering wheel stood the gray-haired man and the blacksmith,

their oilskins flapping, dripping with spray. The gray-haired man shouted something, but the whistling of the wind in the rigging and the banging of the leeboard were too loud for his shout to be understood.

Inside, the ship was wonderfully warm. All the bunks were empty and neatly made and the hospital was very tidy, but it looked like the Crazy House in a fair, for everybody had to walk leaning sideways. The cook came out with two paper mugs with cocoa, but before they had been able to drink it, the door to the hospital was torn open and Sparks came down, crabwise. "The children have to come out on deck with life-belts on!" he called to the sister. "Orders from Mr. Tadema."

"Christmas!" the sister exclaimed, alarmed. "Are we going down?"

Sparks grinned. "Not yet," he said, "but Mr. Tadema wants to make sure they'll float free of the wreckage if we do."

"Is there any danger?" the sister asked; Cook peered over her shoulder like a worried dog.

"Not the slightest," Sparks said, "but if I were you, I would do as he says. He's very nervous. I'll get you the lifebelts."

He staggered toward the front of the ship, and came back with two lifebelts which he put on the children. They were frightened, for the waves now slammed against the side of the ship, exploded into spray and burst against the big windows with a violent noise. As Sparks sat tying the tapes on the life-belts, Sister asked, "Why on earth do we have to sail? Why didn't he put the engine on?"

"Our draught is less than four feet," Sparks answered, "so we can't have the engine on when there are waves. The propeller would be out of the water most of the time and the engine would burst its guts. He'll put it on as soon as we are in the lee of the dike. At least, I suppose he will." Then he lifted the children off the bunk and said, "All right, out you go. Hold on to me, I'll take you there."

When the children came out on deck, the wind caught them and knocked their breath away. Three men were standing at the wheel now, pulling with all their might, the blacksmith, Mr. Tadema and the judge. Over their heads, the white flag with the red cross was stretched out taut. They looked strange and wild with their wet hair matted on their foreheads, their oilskins glistening with spray. The sea was white-capped and angry; dark, ragged clouds sailed low over the water, and in the vast emptiness many ships could be seen laboring, throwing up showers of spray. They all had their flags at half-mast to honor the dead of the flood, the colors looked gay in the grayness.

The children huddled together in the lee of the superstructure, and they saw with rising alarm the edge of the ship's deck trail through the water every time the wind pushed it on its side. The waves that boiled past were green and transparent, flecked with foam and gutted with whirlpools; they clutched the handrail and watched the turbulent water swirl past their feet with horrible fascination. They had never seen the sea from so close; it frightened them for the first time. Until then they had seen its fury and its strength only from a distance; it had never assaulted them. During that hour, on the slanting deck, they came to know the terror of the floods that had changed the grownups around them.

When at last the ship entered the shelter of a broken dike and the waves abated, Sparks came to pick them up and they were put back inside. On one of the bunks in the hospital, Miss Winter was lying, her eyes closed. Overhead, the sails came down with the noise of a house caving in, and Adinda took Jan's hand. Miss Winter moaned and stirred. They sat close together on the edge of their bunk in their lifebelts, and heard the engine throb to life. The hospital started trembling, then it began to shake; the windows rattled, the lamps clattered and the tier of bunks started squeaking all around them. Sparks came back, looked at them thoughtfully with an absent-minded grin and said, "You like it better outside, I suppose?"

The children said nothing; they just stared at him.

"All right," he said, "come on out. We're entering the harbor."

He took them outside once more. There was only one man at the wheel now, a stranger. Behind the ship, a small rowing boat bobbed up and down, attached to them with a rope. As they looked ahead, they saw they were heading for a gap in the dike; a thin row of dead treetops sticking out of the muddy water led up to it. Through the gap, they saw a glimpse of a quayside and houses; a church tower and a windmill looked at them over the top of the dike.

The water had changed. It was still turbulent and wild, but there were no more waves. The ship crept forward into a fierce muddy current. Bits of wreckage swirled past: broken chairs, mattresses, whole islands of floating onions. As they slowly edged nearer the gap, the air also changed. It began to smell, sweet and sickly. Stacks of hay came drifting past; the stranger at the wheel shouted, "Send two men out front with poles, to clear the channel!"

"What's this current?" Mr. Tadema called.

"Tide's changing," the stranger answered, "and the lock is broken. This is water running out of the polder. Can you put on some more speed?"

Mr. Tadema looked at the blacksmith, who frowned and

shook his head. "I wouldn't," he grunted. "If I give her more, she'll blow her top."

The ship was slowly swinging round now, following a bend in the line of dead treetops. Then, suddenly, a horn blasted behind the dike and a gray ship shot out of the gap, pushing a white-capped wave in front of it with its bow, on which the number *UK 602* was painted. Mr. Tadema shouted, jumped at the wheel, stumbled, scrambled to his feet again, grabbed a little trumpet and blew two shrill squeaks, his cheeks bursting, his eyes bulging. The pilot spun the wheel, the ship veered, and the *UK 602* scraped past them without reducing speed; in its wheelhouse a fur-capped giant stood gaily waving. Mr. Tadema gave a sound like a sob, and sat down on the steps to the wheel, his head in his hands. The pilot cursed, shook his fist at the vanishing ship and spun the wheel again. They slowly crawled on toward the gap in the dike, through the wreckage, the onions, the drifting hay, until they veered once more and nosed in through the gap.

It had been a lock once; now its doors hung splintered and broken in their hinges, and the water gushed in a torrent between the walls. The ship shuddered and squeaked as the engine raced faster; they slowly crept up the torrent, the explosions of the exhaust echoing deafeningly against the walls of the lock.

When at last they were through, they entered the ruin of a harbor. The quayside was shattered and covered with rubble: furniture, dead cattle, upturned carts, splintered staircases. There were fires with people around them, warming their hands. In front of the first house, staring at them with empty windows, lay a rusty ship stranded on top of the quay. A steel cable had been looped around it and stretched taut across the fairway to the other side, where some men were busy with a winch.

The pilot took the trumpet and gave three squeaks; there was a lot of shouting while the ship was swung round by the current; then the men let down the cable. It vanished in the water, the ship started trembling once more, and crept on past the wrecked quayside. They only saw the tops of the houses that followed, for against their gables a wall of coffins had been stacked up. The smell they had noticed outside became thicker. Then the children saw the houseboat.

It was moored against the sunken hull of a fishing smack; a row of narrow planks led from the front door to a white, sandy gap in the quayside. They danced up and down on the deck, shouting, "There's our houseboat! Look, look! There's our houseboat!" Sparks called, "Ssh!" for behind the houseboat, a small procession passed of five coffins carried by sailors in blue overalls and high boots, and followed by a small band of mourners led by two old men in black cloaks. The children screamed, "Father! Father! Hey, Father!" and one of the old men looked up. He hesitated a second, then he stood stock-still, waved delightedly and was pushed on by the people following behind. The children danced up and down again, waving wildly. Jan shouted, "There he goes! There he is! Please, mister, put us ashore! Please, please!" Sparks said, "Ssh! Ssh! We'll put you ashore in a minute. Now don't call any more, your father is busy."

They moored a few minutes later, behind the sunken vessel and the houseboat. Sailors caught the mooring ropes that were flung ashore, and as the ship slowly edged toward the quay, the children screamed "Bos'n! Hey, bos'n! Hallo, hallo! Bos'n!"

A sailor on the quay stared at them, frowned, then his face broke into a grin and he waved back, shouting, "Hallo there! Hallo! I've got something for you!" He gave an order to the other sailors handling the ropes, then he clumped away in his heavy boots and vanished in one of the houses behind the coffins. The ship was moored when he came back, carrying a basket. "Come and look!" he called from above, squatting on the edge of the quay. "I've got a surprise for you!"

Mr. Tadema's nervous voice cried, "Nobody is to go ashore! Keep those children on board!" But already Sparks and the judge had lifted them up; the bos'n and the freckled sailor had caught their outstretched arms and pulled them onto the quay. "Hallo, children! Hallo!" the bos'n said, rubbing his face against theirs and putting his big arms around them. It seemed incredible that they had parted only yesterday; he had almost a beard now and he smelled like a goat. Adinda threw her arms around his neck and kissed him while Jan hugged the freckled sailor; then the bos'n said, "Look!" and took them to the basket. They bent over it, awkwardly because of their lifebelts, the lid squeaked open and there sat Prince, cowering and bedraggled, glaring at them maliciously with one golden eye. "Well," said the bos'n, "what do you . . ." He stared after them, his mouth open, as they ran away as fast as their legs could carry them, jumping over the rubble on the quay, until the white specks of their lifebelts vanished among the coffins.

They caught up with the funeral procession on the outskirts of the village. They had stumbled among wreckage, scurried through the stinging smoke of fires, and left the motionless tramps who stood warming their hands staring after them with stupefied eyes. The cortege was slowly climbing the slope of the dike as they struggled, panting, past the mourners until they reached the old men in the black cloaks. They grabbed Mr. Grijpma's hands, calling "Father! Father!" jumping up to be kissed. He bent down without stopping, kissed them, hugged them; he too smelled like a goat, and his face was silvery with stubble. "Darlings, darlings," he said. "Ssh! How wonderful! How splendid! Ssh! Where do you come from, I mean, ssh! Let's walk quietly. Ssh, now. In a minute we'll—I mean—ssh!" He led them by the hand, and they solemnly followed the file of coffins. The other old man smiled down at them shyly. He looked very dirty and carried a prayerbook too, like Mr. Grijpma. He wore spectacles which seemed to bother him.

The sailors' boots squeaked, their steps squelched in the mud and the children marched behind, proud and happy. Then Mr. Grijpma asked, in a whisper, "Where's your mother? Have you seen her?"

Jan whispered back, "She's in the tower, I think she's dead, but we've got all the animals. They're on board the hospital ship now, and the bos'n has got Prince, but we don't . . ."

Mr. Grijpma said, "Ssh!" again, and he pressed their hands.

They slowly walked on in silence; when they reached the crown of the dike the wind caught them, but the lifebelts kept them warm. The procession stopped at a big, dark hole in the dike, with a mound of wet clay beside it. The sailors put down the coffins, looped ropes around them and lowered them one by one. The mourners formed a huddled group behind them; some of them sniffed, and the sailors whispered warnings to one another as one of the coffins slipped.

When they were all down, Mr. Grijpma opened his Bible, and read, "Save me, O God; for the waters are come in unto my soul. I sink in deep mire, where there is no standing; I am come into deep waters, where the floods overflow me."

There was a sound of shots, and while Mr. Grijpma read on imperturbably, the children saw a panting little dog run up the dike, followed by a soldier in a white helmet, shooting with his revolver. Behind him an old couple came running; the man shouted, "Don't! Don't! He is ours!" Another shot rang out; Mr. Grijpma's voice chanted calmly, "I am weary of my crying: my throat is dried: mine eyes fail while I wait for my God. My prayer is unto thee, O Lord; in the multitude of thy mercy, hear me."

The soldier stooped down, picked up the still little dog, carried it to the edge of the dike and threw it into the water. The old couple turned round, and walked slowly back toward the village. The soldier caught up with them; they walked away together, talking.

"Deliver me out of the mire, and let me not sink," Mr. Grijpma chanted. "Let not the waterflood overflow me, neither let the deep swallow me up, and let not the pit shut her mouth upon me. Hear me, O Lord; for thy lovingkindness is good: turn unto me, according to the multitude of thy tender mercies. And hide not thy face from thy servant; for I am in trouble: hear me speedily. Amen."

Then he stepped back. The other old man stepped forward, opened his book, shoved his spectacles up his nose and started to chant in Latin. The children stood proudly by Mr. Grijpma's side, their hands in his, their flushed faces beaming above the lifebelts. When the other old man had chanted "Amen" in his turn, they jumped up at Mr. Grijpma once more, and he hugged them again and kissed them.

They went back to the village, together with the other old man, who had now taken off his spectacles and stepped into puddles all the time, which seemed to make him giggle. "So these are your dear little children?" he said, shaking his foot to get the mud off. "Well, well, every day has its little miracle."

Mr. Grijpma said, "This is Father Ambrosius, a colleague of mine. We live together in Mrs. Ool's houseboat for the present. Say hello to him nicely, children."

The children gave the old man a limp hand each, which he

pressed uncertainly. He looked at Adinda shortsightedly and said, smiling, "My, don't you look healthy!"

Jan said, "She's a Negro," and Mr. Grijpma said, "Nonsense. Tell me, children, where on earth have you been?"

They told him, as they walked back to the village. Jan told the story, but he lied so shamelessly that Adinda had to interrupt him all the time. They passed the fires and the coffins; Father Ambrosius, smiling all the time, nodded in all directions, he even nodded at a lamppost. Mr. Grijpma said, "Put your spectacles back on, colleague," and Father Ambrosius answered, "I will in a minute, thank you. I'm just giving my eyes a rest. Why do they insist on printing prayerbooks in such small type, I wonder?" Mr. Grijpma called, "Watch out!" but already Father Ambrosius stood ankle deep in a puddle, his skirts lifted. As he squelched out, he said, "Maybe you're right. I used to walk through this village for hours, without ever . . ." Then he put his spectacles back.

When they arrived at the houseboat, the two old men stood at the gangplank for minutes on end, saying, "After you," and "No, no, after you," while shots rang out in the village. In the end, Mr. Grijpma went first, leading Father Ambrosius by the hand who, in his turn, led Adinda. As they entered, the children noticed that the houseboat had changed. The bird cage was empty and the ship smelled oppressively of feet. The sitting room was very untidy. On the small table in front of the fireplace, a newspaper was spread out full of crumbs, with on it half a loaf, a greasy saucer with butter, a pot of jam with a knife in it and a half-chewed cigar. Bits of string had been strung across the room from one curtain rod to the other, and from it hung three black socks with blue darns and a pair of Jaeger combinations.

"Well, welcome to our little abode," Father Ambrosius said, bumping into a chair. "What shall I make you for a festive cup of reunion? Some sweet lime?"

"If you will, colleague," Mr. Grijpma said. "That's very kind of you. Are there some clean cups left?"

"Oh, never mind, never mind," Father Ambrosius said. "I think this is a wonderful opportunity to do the washing up."

"No, no," said Mr. Grijpma, getting up from the couch. "I won't let you do the washing up alone, I . . ."

Father Ambrosius held up two grimy hands in a gesture of blessing, while Jan looked round the room, wondering where the fourth sock was. "No question of it," he said. "You sit here nice and intimate with your dear little children while I wash the crockery. What else can I give you? Some . . . er . . . jam?"

"We are quite happy, colleague," Mr. Grijpma said. "Why don't you just lie down for a few minutes? You'll have to go back into the polder in an hour's time, and last night . . ."

"No question of it," Father Ambrosius said, giggling. "I'll make you a nice cup of something." Then he shuffled away, tripping up on the threshold.

Mr. Grijpma looked at the children with tired blue eyes and smiled. He put out his hand and said, "Come and sit down beside me."

"You need a wash," Adinda said. "Are these your combinations?"

"No, no," said Mr. Grijpma. "Come, sit down and . . . tell me what happened, I mean . . . just tell me."

"But we told you everything," Jan said. "So we hid in a coffin and then we came out when the ship was at sea and we put on lifebelts and sailed here in a terrible storm and then we saw you."

[153]

"Yes, yes," Mr. Grijpma said, pressing their hands, "but I mean . . . what exactly happened to Mother?"

The children glanced at one another, then Jan said, "She stayed in the tower."

Mr. Grijpma said, "I see," and pressed their hands again. "But was she . . . I mean . . . are you sure she was . . ."

Adinda said, "Yes, otherwise we wouldn't have left her."

Mr. Grijpma said, "I see," again, and looked at her with a smile, biting his lip.

"She was quite all right," Jan said. "When I last saw her, she was smiling."

Adinda shot him a black glance, but when Mr. Grijpma asked, "Ah?" she calmly said, "Yes."

"What happened to you?" Jan asked, and when Mr. Grijpma said, "Pardon?" he repeated his question. "Oh, I was on my way to the dike," Mr. Grijpma said, "and just as I was at the harbor, the water came and I somehow managed to climb on board a ship that was on its way to pick up people off the roofs in Queen Street."

"We saw you!" Jan cried. "We saw you from the belfry. You sent out a little boat."

Mr. Grijpma said, "That's right."

"Wasn't it sunk by a house that fell on top of it?" Adinda asked.

Mr. Grijpma said, "That's right."

"And then?" Jan urged. "What happened then? How did you get to Onderkerk?"

"Well," said Mr. Grijpma, tiredly, "that is a long story. But the gist of it is that the ship ran aground and . . . and got into trouble, and then some Urker fishermen picked us up and brought us here. I stayed behind."

[154]

There was a loud rumbling noise outside as someone ran down the gangplank; then there was a knock at the door. Mr. Grijpma got up and went to the hall; the children heard Father Ambrosius say, "No, no, colleague, don't bother. I will," and Mr. Grijpma, "Nonsense. I'm there already. Please don't trouble yourself." The front door was opened and a gruff voice asked, "Are the children here?" Mr. Grijpma answered timidly, "Yes, er . . . Sergeant." The gruff voice said, "Here, that's from the bos'n. Better watch out. It's dynamite."

Mr. Grijpma came back, frowning, carrying a basket. He muttered, "Dynamite? What on earth . . ."

Adinda bit her knuckles and Jan hid behind her back as Mr. Grijpma put the basket down and stretched out his hand to open the lid.

"Don't!" Jan cried. "If you let him out, we'll never get him back in again!"

Mr. Grijpma looked up, nonplused. "Pardon?"

"It's Prince," said Jan. "Prince is in there."

Mr. Grijpma said, "Ah," and stood looking at the basket.

"Perhaps he'll be nice now," Adinda said tentatively, watching Mr. Grijpma's face.

Then Father Ambrosius came in, carrying a tray with two cups and a jam pot filled with tea. "I don't seem to find the third cup," he said, "so if you don't mind roughing it. . . ."

Then Mr. Grijpma opened the lid and Prince sprang out. He ran round the sitting room, hissing; then he went for Father Ambrosius, and got entangled in his skirts.

It took them quite some time to collect the cups and the pieces of the broken jam jar; then they managed to lock Prince in the bedroom, while Mr. Grijpma sat quietly crying underneath the combinations.

Toward nightfall, Mr. Tadema came. Father Ambrosius had made some new beverage, and they sat sipping it with narrowing mouths, while outside the wild day was dying.

Mr. Tadema was very kind. His nervousness seemed to have gone, now that they had arrived in Onderkerk; for the first time he looked at the children with sympathy. He brought out a notebook in which he jotted down their names, their ages, where they came from and where they intended to go. Mr. Grijpma said he wasn't quite sure yet, but he thought he had heard that all evacuees from Niewerland were sent to Elburg, where it so happened that an old friend of his student days was parson. So he thought they would all go there to wait for the water to go down; he would go back to Niewerland with the first settlers and take the children with him.

He was very attached to the children, more so than he had

ever shown. He sat with them on the couch, his arms around them, and every time they stirred he hugged them, as if he were afraid they would go away. When Mr. Tadema suggested that the children should sleep on board the hospital ship, he refused to let them go at first. Father Ambrosius convinced him, for the only place where they could sleep was on the floor. Mr. Tadema promised they would be back in the morning; when he took them with him, Mr. Grijpma kissed them with tears in his eyes and said, "I'll come in later to say good night to you." As they edged sideways up the springy gangplank, he stood in the doorway of the houseboat, waving; Father Ambrosius appeared behind him, put his hand on his shoulder and gently drew him inside.

When they walked along the edge of the quayside toward the hospital ship, wheels rattled past them and they saw a long horse-drawn trailer, loaded with dead animals, accompanied by Marines with torches, fierce and unearthly in the dancing light. The Marines were laughing and joking; on the cart were a horse, two cows, a number of pigs, some sheep, a hare and a toy elephant. At the gangplank of the hospital ship, a file of soldiers and sailors were waiting. As they passed them, Mr. Tadema asked, "What are you boys waiting for?" and one of them answered, "A bath."

Inside, most of the bunks were occupied by noisy patients, who flustered Miss Winter as she darted from bed to bed. They were all unshaven, and smoking; when Sister came in, they hid the cigarettes in the palms of their hands.

"Where shall we put the children, Sister?" Mr. Tadema asked.

"In the nursery," Sister answered curtly; then she asked, "Who is smoking in here?"

Nobody answered. Cook came up the dining-room stairs,

carrying Ko and Bussy, and Noisette ran between the bunks, her tail up. A man with a red beard pointed at her, calling, "Tatatatatat!" imitating a machine gun; Sister snapped, "Stop that! Finish with your bedpan instead of behaving like a lout!"

"All cats have to be shot," the man with the red beard said somberly.

"Why, for heaven's sake?" Sister asked.

"Because they are members of the Mau Mau," the man answered. All the patients laughed, and Sister said, "Come on, children! Wash your hands in the kitchen, have your meal and then off to bed."

"There's a whole queue outside waiting to take a bath," Mr. Tadema said.

Sister answered, "I know. I'm putting them through two at a time. We take those who handle the corpses first."

The children went down to the kitchen to wash their hands. The dining room was full of soldiers with pink faces, each of them with a little glass in his hand. The judge, Sparks and the blacksmith were sitting among them; in the far corner sat two civilians, a man with glasses and a woman in a jersey with a muffler knotted round her neck. They were smoking and laughing.

When the children came back to eat the sandwiches Cook had put down for them, the woman stared at them and burst into tears, her head on the table. There was an embarrassed silence, while the man with the glasses stroked her hair. Then the judge said, lightly, "But on the whole, the work you're doing must give you, well, satisfaction?"

"Of course," a sailor said. "Someone has to do it, so it might as well be us. It isn't too bad, as long as you don't look at their faces from below. That's what I told the ones that arrived today: only look at them from above, then it isn't too bad."

"I had one old woman today," a Marine said, "who held a tuft of reeds in one hand and a Bible in the other. I must say that shook me. She looked very fierce."

"Here," said the judge to the woman, who had looked up and wiped her eyes with her muffler. "Have another drink."

"I don't think I will," she said shakily, with a smile. "I think it's the drink that does it. I wouldn't mind another cigarette, though." Four people held out a packet to her, and she laughed as she chose one. After someone had lit her cigarette for her, she sighed and said, "Ah, this is lovely. How old are you, children?"

Adinda said, "I'm eleven and he's ten."

"Well, well," she said, then her lips started to tremble.

The judge asked quickly, "And what do you do with the animals?"

"Those we can get at, we collect," the Marine said. "We stack them at the far end of the dike, and there they are destroyed with flame-throwers. In other places, they ship them to some factory to make soap or something, but here they can't be shipped because no ship can get at us."

Two more sailors came down the steps, their faces shining, their damp hair neatly combed. "Boy!" said one of them, "I feel another man! Never knew a bath could make so much difference."

"Sit down," said the judge. "We can still make some room for you, I think."

"Don't bother, sir," the sailor said. "We'll sit on the stairs. We've been sleeping on benches for four nights, so . . ."

"That's the trouble," said the Marine who had talked about

the animals. "We don't mind sleeping in the open if it can't be avoided, but do you know that there's a whole stack of hay, nice and dry, just behind the farm with the old man in it? We asked the burgomaster if we could put it in one of the rooms of the Town Hall to sleep on, but he said it would make too much mess."

"Oh, that bastard!" a soldier said. "He ought to be shot! Do you know that he wanted to put a policeman with us in the boats to see that we didn't pinch anything? People like him make me see red."

"Of course, no one thinks of your doing any looting unless he's out of his mind," the judge said appeasingly, "but I believe there has been looting in some places."

"There has been here," said a big Marine who had been sitting quite still in his corner so far, without speaking. "Yesterday a civilian came off the waterboat with a parcel for the doctor. He was wearing a Red Cross armband, so we let him through. What was in that parcel, Doctor?"

The man with the glasses said, "Pardon?"

"That little civilian," the Marine repeated, "who came in with a parcel for you. About thirty-five, thin hair, blue eyes, gray pinstripe suit, brown shoes, very muddy. A parcel about that big."

"I didn't see him," the doctor said. "No one had a parcel for me."

"I'm not surprised," said the Marine. "It probably had some old newspapers inside. He must have thrown it away once he was out of sight. We shot him this morning."

There was a silence; then the judge asked, "Why was that?"

"We saw him bent over the corpses, that were laid out on the dike waiting to be taken to the morgue," the Marine answered.

"At first, we thought he belonged to the identification committee because of his armband. Then he looked up, saw us and ran away. When we came to the corpses, we saw that fingers were cut off. He ran to the end of the dike; when he reached the gap and couldn't go any farther, he ran back toward us and went for us, so we shot him. He had five rings in his pocket. He was buried this afternoon with the others. His name will probably be on a monument some day, as a victim of the flood."

The silence that followed was broken by Sister's voice, calling from upstairs: "Come on, children! To bed! It's getting late."

Adinda got off her chair and said politely, "Good night, everybody." Everybody said, "Good night." As they were led toward the door at the far end of the hospital, Adinda said, "Good night, everybody" again, and the patients called, "Good night! Sleep well!" In the doorway, Jan screamed, "Good night, everybody!" The sister shook him by the shoulder and said, "Ssh!" hastily shutting the door behind her. Miss Winter came out of the bathroom in a cloud of steam, her hair bedraggled and her apron wet. "I'm very sorry, Sister," she said, hysterically, "but I don't think I'm the right person to put these—these men in the bath."

"Come, come," Sister said, "don't be foolish, Miss Winter."

"I am not!" Miss Winter cried. "I'm willing to do anything, anything at all, I've come to help, but not to let perfectly healthy young beasts take liberties with me!"

"All right, Miss Winter," Sister said. "You put these children to bed and I'll take over." She breezed into the bathroom, was greeted hilariously; then there was the sound of two resounding slaps, she was heard to say, "Show me your ears!" and the door was pulled shut.

Miss Winter took the children into a small room next to the bathroom, where the animals welcomed them joyously. It was decorated with rabbits and teddy bears; gold paper stars were glued to the ceiling, and there were two small bunks let into the wall with bars in front, like playpens. They were put to bed; Adinda was given Noisette and Jan Ko and Bussy; then Miss Winter took a book and read aloud in a strained voice, "The first time Ferdinand played with Puss was in a haystack . . ." A shout of laughter sounded behind the thin wall that separated them from the bathroom. Sister's voice called out, "That's enough of that! Out you go! Next two!" Miss Winter sobbed and ran out, hiding her face with her apron. Jan shouted "Good night!" at the wall, and two voices behind it yelled back, "Good night!"

Then Sister came in briskly, said, "I don't want to hear another sound out of you, or I'll put you with the cook!" She put the bars in front of their bunks, turned out the light and went away. The children lay listening to the splashing, the singing and the guffawing behind the wall until they fell into a fitful slumber.

They were woken up because the light was turned on again, and there was Mr. Grijpma, looking guilty, with a thin rolled-up mattress under his arm, a pillow and a blanket.

"Are you sure you'll be all right?" a voice asked behind him, and he said, "Oh, absolutely, Mr. Tadema. It's only because, well, I'm afraid Father Ambrosius is rather a noisy sleeper and . . . well, good night."

"Good night, sir," Mr. Tadema's voice said. "Sleep well."

Mr. Grijpma gave a self-conscious little laugh, then he shut the door behind him, listened at it, tiptoed to the center of the room with creaking shoes and rolled out the mattress. Through the bars of the bunks, the children and the animals watched him. There was no chair in the room, so he sat down on the mattress to take off his shoes. As he sat there with one foot on his knee, he looked up and saw the children. "Ssh," he said, "you're supposed to be asleep."

"Don't you wash?" Adinda asked.

Mr. Grijpma frowned. "I suppose I may be allowed to undress first," he said, "or do you want me to wash with my clothes on?"

"Will you let us out?" Jan asked. "Will you tell us a story?"

"I will if you are very quiet," Mr. Grijpma said, "and if you give me a chance to make my bed first."

They watched him while he undressed until he stood in his underwear. He put his socks in his shoes, opened the door and put them outside; then he went to the wash basin in the corner, wetted his hands, rubbed his eyes with them, dried his face, gargled and made his bed. He made it very tidily, tucking in the blanket; then he went back to his clothes, felt in all the pockets, found a dirty handkerchief, blew his nose in it and put it underneath the pillow.

Adinda, behind her bars, asked, "Is that all you do?"

Mr. Grijpma eyed her sternly and said, "Fresh water is very scarce in this village, and that's quite enough from you, thank you. Well, all right, I'll let you out; but only for a moment."

He undid the hooks and took away the bars in front of the bunks; then he lifted Jan out of the top one; when Jan cried, "Bussy! Take Bussy out, or he'll fall!" he lifted Bussy out too. "And Ko?" Jan asked, when he was put down. "Ko is still up there!" Mr. Grijpma groped in the bunk and brought out Ko by his ears. Bussy squatted in a corner, but they all behaved as if they did not see it. Mr. Grijpma got into his bed and then he said, "If you're very quiet and promise to go back when I tell you, you may come under the blanket with me for a minute. Let's say this is a Sunday."

They got under the blanket, one on each side, and put their heads on his shoulder. Adinda said, "Oof poof!"

Mr. Grijpma asked, "What's the matter?"

"She thinks you smell," Jan said, "as if she didn't smell herself. She talks about washing all the time, but just let her get a whiff of herself."

Mr. Grijpma said, "Children, children! I've missed you very much, I even doubted that we would ever see one another again, and now we're lying here together, thanks to God's infinite mercy, I don't want to talk about how we smell. I want us to be grateful and happy and, well, at peace."

Bussy came back and sniffed at his hair. He rolled up his eyes and put his head back to see him; then Bussy licked his nose, which made him sneeze. Adinda groped underneath the pillow and gave him the dirty handkerchief. He blew his nose with his arm around Jan's neck, and Adinda put the handkerchief back again.

"Are we going to stay together now?" Jan asked.

Mr. Grijpma said, "Yes, God willing."

"Are you going to take another wife?"

Mr. Grijpma said, "I—I don't think so."

"Is Father Ambrosius going to stay with us?" Adinda asked.

"I don't think so."

"Did you and he call one another names when you first met?" asked Jan.

"Why?"

"A boy from Volendam called me a Protestant midget, and then an Urker threw a lump of earth at him."

"Well," said Mr. Grijpma, carefully, "the miracle that God

has brought about with this flood is that He has made us realize that we are all human beings, dependent on one another, and that our God is the same. I wouldn't mind living with Father Ambrosius. I wouldn't mind a bit, but I'm afraid that in a week or so, when the worst is over, that may become difficult again. That's why I want you to keep your ears and your eyes wide open, to see and to hear the miracle while it lasts."

"I've seen a lot of it already," Jan said. "I saw a flying lantern with a Negro inside with a yellow cap on, and I saw a boat on wheels."

"That's wonderful," Mr. Grijpma said, "but it's not quite what I mean. I mean this: hasn't everybody you've met since the flood been very kind to you?"

"Oh, yes," said Adinda.

Jan said, "We've got so many friends now; we've got the bos'n, and the Urkers, and Sparks, and the blacksmith, and Sister . . ."

"Not Sister," Adinda said. "Miss Winter."

Jan said, "Pooh! Miss Winter is silly."

Adinda said, "You're silly yourself."

"Children, children," Mr. Grijpma said, "that's not what I mean at all. If what I say is too difficult for you, I'll stop talking about it; but I don't think it is, if you'll just be quiet and peaceful and listen to me."

"I'm listening," Adinda said. "I know what you mean."

"Well, what do I mean?" Mr. Grijpma asked.

"Everybody has been frightened," Adinda said, "and they're always nice just afterward."

Mr. Grijpma said, "Hm. Yes. I suppose that's right. But, you see, here in this broken village, with all those dead people and dead animals around us, there is a wonderful feeling just now of all mankind helping, and, well, thinking of us with love. Do you know that everybody all over the world has sent us clothes and shoes and money? I found some Spanish coins in a suit that was dropped by the Red Cross, and Father Ambrosius found a note in French in another suit, that came out of the same parcel. We kept that note, for to us it expressed the heart of the miracle. It said, '*Notre race c'est l'humanité, notre patrie le monde.*' "

"What does that mean?" Adinda asked.

"Our race is mankind, and our fatherland the world."

"Your race is white," Adinda said, "and your fatherland is Holland."

Mr. Grijpma shook his head. "No," he said.

"I haven't got a race," Adinda said. "I haven't got a fatherland either, but I don't care."

Noisette cautiously walked up Mr. Grijpma's legs, sinking into the blanket. She sat down on his stomach and began to wash herself.

"Maybe you are a very fortunate girl," Mr. Grijpma said. "You are ahead of all of us, and when you are bigger, I think that there may be a wonderful task for you, helping to make the races and the peoples of the world forget about their fatherlands, and understand one another."

Suddenly, Adinda kissed him on the cheek; Noisette lost her balance and stalked away.

"Do you understand a little of what I mean?" Mr. Grijpma asked.

Adinda whispered, "Ssh! Jan's asleep."

Mr. Grijpma said, "Ah." Then he whispered, "I think I'd better put you to bed now."

Adinda said, "Ssh," again, got up and tucked them both

in. Then she lifted Ko, Noisette and Bussy into Jan's bunk, and put the bars in front. She tiptoed to the light switch; as she stood with her hand on it, she whispered, "Good night."

Mr. Grijpma whispered, "Good night."

She turned off the light and went back to her bunk in the darkness. Behind the partition the bath was running once more.

From time to time in the night the children were half awakened by the sound of bath water running, and the singing and shouting next door went on until dawn. The engine for the water pressure switched on and off constantly; at dead of night there was a loud crunching and banging, and the ship shuddered as another vessel moored alongside. It was the waterboat, for shortly afterward they heard a loud gushing noise as a powerful jet of water thundered down into a tank under the floor of their cabin.

When at last they were woken up in the morning by Cook coming in with three paper mugs of tea, Mr. Grijpma told them to dress very quickly for they had to be in time for the roll call in the village square. Jan asked what a roll call was, and Mr. Grijpma explained, as he dressed, that ever since the flood the population of the village had to line up every morning at seven o'clock, to answer when their names were called out by the burgomaster; then they were given their rations of bread, butter and jam; they had to be back in the village square at midday and at five o'clock at night with a pan to collect their hot meal from the communal kitchen.

Mr. Tadema came to call them, saying that they should hurry up; every civilian on board had to call at the Town Hall to get identity papers before the roll was called.

When they went ashore, with Mr. Tadema and all the crew except the doctor, they found Father Ambrosius waiting for them. He looked even dirtier than the day before, his cassock was caked with mud up to his knees and there was a big tear on his hip, pinned up with a safety pin, showing his underwear. He held out a podgy hand, keeping his spectacles on his nose with the other as he bent down. After they had gingerly shaken hands with him he said to Mr. Grijpma, "I'm afraid poor Farmer Pos is quite mad now. I went there last night with the Navy, but he threatened us with his pitchfork and we didn't dare go up the ladder. His wife and three little children are in a very poor condition, so I thought of a little plan which I'd like to discuss with you before I mention it to the gentleman who owns the hospital ship. . . ."

The children didn't listen, for there was a lot to see. As they slowly walked on along the gutted quayside, there were, at first, just the empty houses, the coffins, the dead cattle and the fires. But then, when they turned a windy corner, they saw a spectacle that made them stand still and gape.

They were standing on the crown of a dike that had once been a street, but all the houses facing the land had crumbled into ruins. All that was left were piles of rubble and broken furniture. Behind those, as far as the eye could see, was a vast flat plain of wreckage, so thick that the water on which it floated could not be seen. It consisted of wood, bedding and onions, dotted everywhere with the bloated bellies of cows. Bits of houses stuck out of it, roofless, showing corners of rooms with pictures and flapping wallpaper. Further on, the broken stumps of street lamps showed where once the roads had been. Among the wreckage, three little boats, with sailors in high rubber boots in them, were cautiously feeling their way; as they walked along, they saw one of them pull something out of the water and hoist it into the boat.

"Watch out, children," Mr. Grijpma said, pulling them aside, "and don't look." He pressed their heads against him, trying to shield their eyes. The thudding of hoofs approached, the creaking of a harness, a slow rattle of wheels; Jan peered between Mr. Grijpma's fingers. He saw a Marine pass, then a horse, straining, then a long flat cart like the one they had seen the night before. A number of shoes stuck out over the edge, but he could not quite see, for Mr. Grijpma pressed his face into his coat.

When the cart had rattled past and they were allowed to look again, Mr. Grijpma took them by the hand once more and they stumbled on over the broken pavement toward the end of the ruined street, where they saw the dark mass of a church. On its walls was the watermark: it had come up above the arched doorway.

In front of the church was a square, full of people. Mr. Tadema and his crew went to a building on the left that had a big stoop in front; Mr. Grijpma, Father Ambrosius and the children joined the crowd. Father Ambrosius took off his spectacles and started nodding again; Mr. Grijpma put his hands on the children's shoulders and pressed them tightly against him.

They seemed to wait for hours among the silent people underneath the leaden sky. Father Ambrosius said he was sure there was snow in the air. Then he started talking about his little plan. The only chance perhaps to coax mad Farmer Pos out of his hayloft was to sail close to his farm with the hospital ship, so that he would see its windows, its cozy interior, and then Father Ambrosius would go to see him in a rowboat again, talk to him once more and then who knows? Mr. Grijpma nodded and said, "I see," hugging the children.

A man in a dirty overcoat with a little beret on and a sheaf of papers in his hand walked through the crowd toward the steps of the church, and started shouting names. While he was shouting, a humming noise approached in the sky and quickly grew into a roar, drowning his voice. The children saw a helicopter come down, and land on the rubble next to the Town Hall. Its glass door was opened and out of it came two men in wind jackets and crash helmets and heavy boots that looked beautifully polished. They had cameras slung around their necks on leather straps, and one of them wore sun glasses. Then a Negro came out with a yellow cap on, and Jan shouted, "There he is! That's our Negro! We know him! Please, Father, may I go and say hello to him?" Mr. Grijpma said, "Ssh!" hugging him, but Jan, after waiting in agony for a few more minutes, could not stand still any longer. He slipped out of Mr. Grijpma's grasp, darted through the crowd, and ran toward the Negro, but when he reached him he stopped, overcome with shyness. The Negro beamed at him, his white teeth flashing, and held out a hand that was white on the inside. "Hello," he said. "*Guten Tag, kleines* boy." Jan didn't dare take the hand but he said, "Do you remember? You looked in through the window when we were in the houseboat, and you waved at us."

The Negro grinned, said, "*Guten Tag! Guten Tag!* Want some

gum?" then he unzipped a pocket of his shiny combinations, stuck two fat fingers inside and brought out what looked like a small piece of cardboard. "Chewing gum," he said, "yumyum! Here, *kleines* boy. Eat! Hum, hum," and he chewed. Jan suspiciously took the piece of cardboard in his hand; the Negro said, "Stick in *kleines* mouth. Hum, hum!" and chewed again. He stuck it in his mouth and chewed. It tasted of peppermint, and he beamed. "Thank you," he said. "Come and see my sister. She's a Negro too." He tried to take the Negro's hand, but the Negro patted him on the head, said, "Good-by, *kleines* boy. *Kostet nichts.* Good-by," and walked away toward the Town Hall. He walked as if his pants were wet.

Jan went back to find Mr. Grijpma, chewing the gum with his mouth open and feeling grown-up. Mr. Grijpma looked at him anxiously, almost in tears, and asked, "Where have you been? If you can't stay with me, I won't take you out again!"

Jan said, "I went to see a friend of mine. He gave me tobacco."

"He gave you what?" Mr. Grijpma asked, aghast.

"Tobacco," Jan replied. "A quid. Look," and he opened his mouth.

Mr. Grijpma peered inside, then he said, "I see," relieved. "Now you stay with me," he added, "if you break away once more, I'll have to ask Mr. Tadema to lock you up."

Jan said, "Look," and showed Adinda his open mouth.

Adinda said, "Lll!"

"All right," said Mr. Grijpma to Father Ambrosius. "I think it's a very reasonable plan. Let's put it up to Mr. Tadema." He dragged the children along until he had caught up with Mr. Tadema; while they slowly walked down the gutted street, they all talked about mad Farmer Pos and his pitchfork. Jan tried to tell Adinda about the Negro, but she wouldn't listen; she stolidly turned her head away; when he took the gum out of his mouth to show it to her, she stuck her tongue out again, clasped Mr. Grijpma's hand with both hers and stared rubbing her face against it, like Noisette. Mr. Grijpma stopped talking and bent down to kiss her; Jan muttered, "Bitch," stuck his gum back in his mouth and started chewing again.

Halfway to the ship, the two men in space suits caught up with them and the one with the sun glasses asked, "Is the captain of the hospital ship among you?" When Mr. Tadema said, "That's me," the man saluted and said, "We're down here under the highest authority to take photographs for the Foreign Press. I hear you may be sailing inland to get a crazy farmer out. Would it be all right if we came along?"

Mr. Tadema said, "No question of it! And who gave you that information?"

The man smiled. It was a chilling smile, because of his sun glasses. "It's our job to know everything," he answered. "I assure you, we won't be any trouble."

"I'm sorry," said Mr. Tadema, "but to start with, I've not decided at all that we shall go, and what's more, the presence of Press photographers is the last thing we want in the circumstances."

"I don't think I made myself quite clear," the man said. "We are not the ordinary type of newshawk. . . ."

"What happened to Prince?" Jan asked. "Is he still in the bedroom?"

Mr. Grijpma said, "Ssh!"

". . . very difficult," Father Ambrosius was saying. "Farmer Pos has always been a difficult man, but now he is quite lost in darkness. I've talked to him twice now; this idea of the hospital ship going there is the only slender hope left."

[173]

"I see your point," the man said, unmoved, "but I'm afraid I'll have to take it up on a higher level." Then he asked Mr. Tadema, "You are sailing under Red Cross orders, I take it?"

Mr. Tadema answered, "I am sailing under no one's orders, and I'll thank you to leave us alone."

"In that case, I'll have inquiries made about the flag you are flying," the man said, and he walked away.

Father Ambrosius said, "I do hope I didn't sound impolite, but Farmer Pos is so suspicious, so obsessed. . . ."

"Don't worry, colleague," Mr. Grijpma said. "If they still don't understand, I'll go and explain it to them."

"No one is to stay ashore!" Mr. Tadema called to the small crowd of his crew. "The ship is sailing at high tide, in two hours' time."

Jan cried, "Look!" and pointed at the first snowflakes floating down.

When they arrived on board ship, it was snowing hard. The children stood at the window overlooking the harbor, behind the bunk with the red-bearded man in it. They looked at the swirling snowflakes, their breaths steamed the windowpane and the man with the red beard drew a cat in it with his finger. Then Sister's voice called, "What are you doing sitting up?" and when she discovered the children, she said, "You naughty little monkeys! Off you go, into the nursery!" She took them by the hand and dragged them to the little room where they had slept that night. They were locked up in there, together with the animals, and after some halfhearted efforts to get out, they started exploring. In a cupboard they found two bottles with flat sides and bent necks which looked like tortoises, and Jan played Inundations with them. Bussy, Ko, Noisette and Adinda were sitting on top of a house; he sailed the bottles toward them, ringing a bell and pulling a handle, then he took them off one by one, sailed them toward a rug in the far corner, hooting his horn and cursing the Navy. Adinda didn't want to be taken off; she sat on her legs with her hands in her lap and said the bottle was too small for her.

After that, Jan thought of playing Helicopter by climbing into the top bunk, spreading a towel over his head, saying, "Brrrr!" and jumping off. The second time he did it, he swallowed his chewing gum and that spoiled everything. He lay down on his bunk, pulling faces at the ceiling, while Adinda sat leafing through *Adventures in a Haystack*.

It was a boring morning, that lasted for hours. Never since the afternoon they sat polishing the silver in the kitchen of the parsonage had they been so bored. When the engine started, Jan jumped out of his bunk and hammered on the door, calling, "Let me out! Let me out!" for he was afraid that Mr. Grijpma would be left behind. After a long time, the key was turned and the door opened by Sparks who said, "Hallo there! What are you doing in here?"

"Sister locked us up," Jan said. "Where are we going?"

"We're going for a little ride," Sparks said, "and I think this is a very nice room. Why don't you stay here and keep quiet?"

"We don't want to stay here," Jan said. "We want to come with you. Where's Father?"

"Your father is on deck with the Catholic priest," Sparks said, "and so is practically everybody else. Shall I take you to Sister?"

"No," said Jan. "We don't want to go to Sister. We want to go with you. Are you going back to your little room with the radio? Please take us with you. We'll be very quiet and play."

"All right," said Sparks, "but I'll hold you to your word."

He took them with him, back to the hospital, and they were

about to slip through the door in the dining room when Sister came out of the kitchen, carrying a trayful of paper mugs. "What does this mean?" she snapped. "Did you let those children out?"

Sparks said, "I'm taking them with me to the aft-cabin."

"On one condition," Sister said, "that they shall not come out on deck. God knows what may happen if they do. It's your responsibility."

"Don't worry," said Sparks. "I'll keep them busy all right," and he hastily pushed them into the corridor.

The small room with the radio was almost dark. In the back were two semicircular little windows, behind which snowflakes were swirling. The children climbed onto the bookshelf underneath the windows and looked out. All they could see through the snow was the gray turbulent wake of the ship, its big rudder, and behind it the pilot's rowboat, which they were towing.

The radio was silent, but the engine of the ship made a lot of noise, and after Sparks had tried to start a shouted conversation, without getting any reply, he gave up. There wasn't anything for the children to play with. All they could do was to sit on their knees on the bookshelf and count snowflakes. Then Jan found out that if he made a humming noise, the ship's vibration made it quiver. Adinda tried it too and they sat humming together. Sparks shouted, "For Christ's sake, shut up!" As they looked round, startled, he smiled insincerely from his armchair and asked, "Can't you play at something else, that's less noisy?"

They didn't answer, and sat glumly looking out of the little windows, their faces pressed against the glass, secretly humming. The snowflakes swirled; after looking at them for a long time, they got dizzy and Jan began to think of being sick. He said, in a small voice, "Sparks, I want to be sick."

Sparks said, sternly, "Oh no, you don't! You want a good hiding."

So Jan started looking through the window once more, staring at the swirling snowflakes, imagining how, when he would be grown up, he would tie Sparks' hands behind his back, attach them to his feet and stab him with his penknife until he died. He liked thinking about that; when Sparks was dead and cut up into little bloody bits, he thought of someone else to truss up and stab to death. He chose Sister; but he left her half-killed, yawned and wished the flood were over, for the first time. He put his forehead against the windowpane, shut his eyes and felt the vibrations of the engine in his head. He imagined he was sitting in a helicopter, the engine roared, and he steered through the clouds with a little steering wheel. When he was big, he would be the driver of a helicopter. So far, he had wanted to be a pirate or a bus driver, but a helicopter was better. He would marry Adinda and beat her if she had one of her moods; when she was nice again and willing to play, he would catch birds for her with his helicopter and bring them home and teach them to talk like the grocer's parrot. The grocer's parrot was a big old bird, with a hooked nose and green and yellow feathers; it sat on the counter in a golden cage crying, "Good morning!" and "Come again!" every time the doorbell tinkled. He suddenly realized that he would never see that shop again, nor the parrot, nor the grocer, who had a wart on his nose and who gave them each a toffee every time they came to collect the groceries. He felt sad at the thought, and he went on thinking of the parrot and the wart and the toffees, trying to force tears into his eyes to show to Sparks and make him sorry, but he couldn't. He tried squinting, but that only gave him a headache; then he tried rubbing one eye to make the other weep, the way Farmer

Bouma had taught them to do when they stood looking at him thrashing the corn and got chaff in their eyes. He forgot about his tears when he thought of Farmer Bouma, and the smell of his stable, and the breathy silence of the munching cows, lined up in the darkness, and the taste of fresh warm milk scooped from the bucket, and the face of the newborn calf called Spotty that could only walk with two legs at a time. It suddenly occurred to him that they might never see all that again, that they were heading for a strange place where there would be no grocer, no parrot, no Farmer Bouma, no Spotty and no Mrs. Grijpma. He thought of her for the first time, and he fearfully looked down the well of the stairs once more; then he quickly jumped off the bookshelf, looked at Sparks and stuck out his tongue.

Sparks eyed him coldly and said, "If you do that again, young man, I'll box your ears for you."

He didn't want to do it, but the well of the tower forced him to. Sparks' hand flew up and smacked deafeningly against his head, then he burst into tears, his face in Sparks' lap.

He wept because of everything: because of Spotty and the parrot and the taste of warm milk and the smell of the haystack, because of the toffees and the belfry and Mrs. Grijpma, because of the boredom, and because it was lovely. In the end it was only lovely, the sadness had gone. He just lay there on his knees, howling in Sparks' lap, feeling the sobs shake him with relish. Then he felt a hand stroking his hair and he looked up, his face streaming. He saw Adinda's black eyes stare at him, seeing everything, and he was suddenly overcome by a blind fury. As he jumped at her, she darted away, and Sparks caught him by the back of his apron. He kicked and screamed and that was lovely too; he heard Sparks calling, "Sister! Jesus

[178]

Christ, Sister!" and that made him sorry, but it was too late. Sister's skirts came rustling down the corridor, her voice asked, "What on earth is the matter?" and then, in a last effort to hold on to it all, to the sadness, the relish, the rage and the importance, he sobbed, pointing at Sparks, "He hit me!"

"Poor boy," Sister said, sarcastically. "If you carry on like that he'll probably hit you again. And when he gets tired, I'll take over."

"That's an unusual statement for a child psychologist," Sparks said. "Does this mean that you are leaving the little bastards with me?"

"That's right," said Sister. "You wanted them in here; well, here they are. And here they'll jolly well stay until I'm ready for them. The old priest has just gone off in the rowboat with Mr. Tadema. I may have my hands full in a minute."

"Go on," Sparks said. "Is Tadema rowing himself?"

"Yes," said Sister, "and jolly well too."

"Are we at Madman's Farm already?" asked Sparks; Sister said, "Ssh!" and rustled out.

Sparks took out his handkerchief and wiped the traces left by the children's noses off the little window; then he peered out of one of them. The children climbed back onto the bookshelf and peered out of the other, but there was nothing to see but the rudder and the swirling snow. The wake had gone, and so had the rowboat. Jan realized only then that the engine was silent.

Sparks climbed up the little ladder and lifted the hatch. As he opened it, snow floated in and Jan tried to catch a snowflake, but however much he tried, every time he opened his hand, there was only water. Then Sparks shut the hatch and came down once more, with snow in his hair and on his shoulders. "If ever

I saw a brave man," he said, "it's that old Father what's-his-name."

"Ambrosius," said Jan. "He wears combinations."

Sparks stared at him and said, "If you think that acting the dear little baby-boy will mellow me after your recent performance, you've got a surprise coming."

Jan grinned at him, his teeth bared, and said, "Penknife."

"Ear trumpet," said Sparks, calmly.

Then Adinda's flat voice came from the bunk, where she was sitting on her legs in her maddening pose of indifference. "What's an ear trumpet for?"

"To put in your ear," Sparks said.

"But why? How do you blow it?"

"You don't blow it," Sparks said. "You put it in your ear when you're deaf, and then people speak into it and you can hear them."

Adinda said, "Oh."

"Come here," said Sparks, "I'll show you." He opened the drawer, took out a sheet of paper, rolled it into a funnel and said, "Come. Turn your ear toward me."

Adinda obeyed, suspiciously. He stuck the funnel in her ear and said, "Now is the time for all good men to come to the aid of the party."

Adinda eyed him coolly and said, "I think you're silly."

Sparks sighed, crushed the paper funnel between his hands with a slap, rolled it into a ball, opened one of the little windows and made a move to throw it out; then he froze. The children stood on tiptoe, to look over his shoulder. They saw, through the swirling snow, the dark rowboat with a woman and three children inside. Then Sparks quickly shut the window, turned round and said, "Now what if you both lay down on Mr.

Tadema's bunk? The one who keeps his eyes shut the longest gets a prize."

"Why can't we look?" Adinda asked. "We've seen lots of people taken off roofs by a boat."

"There isn't anything to see," Sparks said, "but do as you please."

They rushed to the bookshelf, climbed onto it and pressed their faces against the windowpane, but there was nothing to see but the rudder, the dark water and the snow. Sparks climbed the ladder again, opened the hatch a crack, steps shuffled overhead and Sister's voice was heard, saying, "Don't cry, my dear, don't cry. You're all right now. It's all over."

A woman's voice sobbed, "Don't let him go back! He'll kill him, he'll kill him!"

Sister's voice said, "Ssh! Don't worry. How old is the little one?" Then came the sound of a door being shut, and Sparks came down the ladder again.

"Well," he said, "what about some music?" and he started twiddling the knobs of the wireless set. There was a humming noise, then a man's voice said, ". . . the injections are free and should be applied for at any Red Cross Post or Red Cross vessel in the area. After the injection, everyone will be given a certificate of immunization, without which access to the flooded areas will be impossible as from zero eight hours this morning, February 6th. I repeat . . ." Sparks said, "Oh, hell," and switched off again.

Jan called, "Look! Look, Sparks! There they go again!" Sparks looked over his shoulder and watched the rowboat with Father Ambrosius and Mr. Tadema vanish in the snow. He put his hand on Jan's shoulder and said, "Tell me what you saw, boy."

Jan looked up at him, amazed. "Mr. Tadema and Father Ambrosius in a rowboat in the snow," he answered.

"That's right," said Sparks, patting his shoulder, "and don't you ever forget it." Then he sighed, looked round the little room with weary eyes, said, "I'm damned if I know what to do with you next. I'm going to sleep." He sat down in his chair, put his feet on the table, his hands behind his head, and closed his eyes.

Jan looked at Adinda, who had climbed back on the bunk and sat staring at her hands in her lap. He walked to her on all fours, said, "Woof!" and as she stared down at him expressionlessly, he said, "Penknife" again, his teeth bared in a grimace. She didn't react, so he climbed into the bunk too, lay down behind her and looked at her plaits from below. He thought of pulling them, then he saw that the hair in the nape of her neck looked like Noisette's fur when she had been out in the rain, and he remembered the animals. "Let's go and get them," he said. "Adinda? Let's go and get the animals."

She shook her head.

He lay thinking of nothing for a while, just words and images: harem, a slice of melon, the dike in the summer, her gooseflesh, the inside of the treble when looked at from below, the well of the tower. He sat up again and pulled her plait. She cried, "Ouch!" and dug him with her elbow. Sparks called, "Peace, peace," without opening his eyes. Then Jan whispered, "Let's sing."

He started, softly, "Little Cart down Sandy Road," and when Adinda did not join in, he nudged her and whispered, "I'll sing the descant."

He started again, and Adinda hummed. He sang louder, delighting in the sound of his own voice, and Adinda started to sing too. They sang it beautifully, better than ever before, and when it was over Jan started "All Ye Prisoners Arise." They were in the middle of it, and it had never sounded so beautiful, when it was all spoiled by the doctor coming in.

He came in hurriedly and said to Sparks, "Can you flash an urgent message on to Scheveningen Radio, to pass on to the Military Commander in Onderkerk?"

"Of course," said Sparks, sitting up. "What's happened?"

"The priest has got him out, but he doesn't want to leave the rowboat. We'll have to tow them, and I want an ambulance or something with some male nurses to be ready for him when we arrive. It's very tricky."

"Is he dangerous?"

The doctor said, "Yes. Can I leave it to you? His children are in bad shape, I'd like to go back to them."

"Of course," said Sparks. "I'll send it straightaway. What time will we be there?"

"I don't know," said the doctor. "Use your common sense. We'll be leaving any minute now," and he hurried away.

Sparks pulled a lever, turned a switch, a blue light flashed on inside the wireless set. He put on his earphones and spoke into the mouthpiece. "Urgent and priority. Urgent and priority. Hospital ship *Honesta* calls Scheveningen Radio. Urgent and priority. Hospital ship *Honesta* calls Scheveningen Radio. Over."

Jan climbed out of the bunk, went to the table and peered at the blue light through the little holes in the side of the wireless set. Inside was a whole engine room of lamps, coils, spirals and colored wires.

"Hospital ship *Honesta* calls Scheveningen Radio," Sparks' voiced droned. "Urgent and priority. Over." The loudspeaker crackled, and a girl's voice came out of it. "Hallo *Honesta*. Hallo

[183]

Honesta. This is Scheveningen Radio. Give me your message. Give me your message. Over."

"Hallo Scheveningen Radio," Sparks said. "Here is a message, urgent and priority, for the Military Commander of Onderkerk, Onderkerk. . . ."

"Hallo *Honesta.* Hallo *Honesta,*" the girl's voice intoned. "Hold on just a minute. Will other ships please stop calling. Will other ships please stop calling. I am taking an urgent message from a hospital ship, and it is very faint. Thank you. Hallo *Honesta.* Hallo *Honesta.* Give me your message slowly please, slowly. Over."

"Hallo Scheveningen Radio," Sparks said, slowly. "I have a message for the Military Commander of Onderkerk, Onderkerk. You'll have to make up the message yourself, I'll just tell you what it is about. We are lying in the flooded area, near a farm about three miles due north of Onderkerk. We have just taken off a farmer and his family, but the farmer is insane and refuses to leave the rowboat in which he is sitting with the priest who brought him out. Now we want an ambulance and some male nurses to be ready for him when we come back, which will be in about an hour's time. Have you got that? He is dangerous. Have you got . . . oh, hell! Of course, there aren't any ambulances in Onderkerk, and they couldn't get one there either. So let's make it a helicopter. Have you got that? A helicopter. Over."

"Ouch!" said Jan. "It's getting all hot, Sparks. Feel!"

Sparks said, "Shut up," and the girl's voice said, "Hallo *Honesta.* Hallo *Honesta.* You have a message urgent and priority for the Military Commander of Onderkerk, Onderkerk. You are due in Onderkerk in one hour's time with a dangerous lunatic, and you want a helicopter and male nurses waiting for you at the quayside. Is that correct? Over."

"Yes, Scheveningen Radio, that is correct. Thank you. Over."

"Hallo *Honesta*, hallo *Honesta*," the girl's voice said. "Does the Military Commander of Onderkerk know the exact place of your arrival, or do you want me to include that in the message? Over."

"They'll know, Scheveningen Radio. They'll know," Sparks said. "Just tell them that we'll moor in the same spot from which we sailed, and they'll know. End of message. Thank you. Over and finish."

"Hallo *Honesta*. Hallo *Honesta*," the girl's voice said. "You'll arrive at your usual mooring place. End of message. Over and finish. Thank you."

Sparks took off his earphones and pulled the lever. The loudspeaker became silent.

"Feel it, Sparks," Jan said. "You can't keep your hand on it."

"I know," said Sparks. "But next time I'm sending a message, shut up. Will you remember that?"

Jan said, humbly, "Yes, Sparks," and he peered into the wireless set again. But all was dark; only a silver lamp glimmered faintly in the far corner.

Then Adinda called, "Look!" and he looked up. She was kneeling on the bookshelf again and peering out of the window. Sparks went to the other one. Jan hastily joined her.

The snow was still swirling, but the dark rowboat had come back. The towrope slanted up toward them again, and in the boat two people were sitting, white and motionless like snowmen. One was Father Ambrosius, his spectacles two white discs, his hand on the knee of the man next to him, who sat with his head bent, holding a pitchfork.

The engine started to throb, the towrope tautened and the rowboat began to move. The man with the pitchfork looked up and Jan jumped down hastily. The man had looked at him in exactly the same way as the one who had jumped at them from the corner of his ruined farm.

"Come, child," Sparks said to Adinda, "don't let's look," and he turned away.

Adinda climbed off the bookshelf, smoothed her skirt and asked, "Is he mata-glap?"

"Pardon?" said Sparks.

"He's going to run amok," Adinda said, "just like old Karto. I'm frightened."

"Well," said Sparks, "so am I. Why don't you lie down and sing again? I liked that."

"What shall we sing?" Jan asked, eagerly. "Onward, Christian Soldiers?"

Sparks nodded, said, "Fine," and Jan lay down on the bunk once more. He started to sing "Onward, Christian Soldiers," but although he nudged Adinda twice, she refused to join in. Then the doctor interrupted him again. He came hurrying in, looking worried. "What are the children doing here?" he asked sternly.

"Sister knows they're here," Sparks answered.

"Out they go," the doctor said. "Quick! And you stay away from the window. Come on, children."

He took them by the hand and led them away. When they reached the hospital, it was strangely silent. Miss Winter sat at the little table in front of the fireplace, her face drawn, her hands clenched. "Where's Sister?" the doctor asked.

"With those children," she said hoarsely.

The doctor muttered, "All right," and took them to the nursery.

The animals were there, and they were very bored. Bussy lay rolled up in a corner, the only corner which he had not wetted. Noisette was asleep on Jan's bunk in an oddly distorted position, one paw outstretched over her ear. Ko sat blinking in the middle of the floor as if he were trying to look at something just in front of his nose. A dotted line of neat little balls ran from Bussy's corner to where he sat.

"Well," said the doctor, "you stay here, children, until Sister comes. She won't be long." Then he shut the door, and they heard him turn the key.

Sister was very long. Darkness began to gather, and they were getting hungry. Although the ship vibrated and rattled with the throbbing of the engine, it was very silent, a silence that frightened them. They climbed into Jan's bunk to look out of the porthole, but there was nothing to see but the swirling snow.

When it was almost dark they were so frightened that they called out, "Sister! Sister!" hammering on the door with their fists.

Cook came in saying, "Hey, hey, hey! What's all the racket?" and when Jan said, "We're hungry," Cook answered, "Now you just wait a couple of hours more and you'll have a lovely meal, all nice and hot from the hay chest."

"I want a sandwich," Jan said. "We haven't had anything to eat since breakfast."

"And I want to go somewhere," Adinda said.

Cook scratched his head, then he said, "Well, all right, but make it quick," and Adinda stiffly walked out of the door, bent double.

[187]

While Cook stood looking after her incredulously, Jan asked, "May I pee in the wash basin?"

Cook said, "Are you out of your mind? Who taught you that?"

"I always do at home," Jan said. "Please, please, Cook. I can't wait."

Cook sighed, said, "Well, I dunno, I suppose. . . . Well, go ahead. But don't tell anybody I said so."

Jan went to the washbasin, but it was too high. "Please, Cook," he asked in his most pleading voice, "please will you lift me up?"

Cook muttered something and lifted him up; then Sister came in. Jan tried to stop, but he couldn't, not even when Cook put him down. He hastily dropped his apron, and started skipping around to hide the growing wet patch.

But Sister didn't notice. She said, "We're arriving. Give me a drink, Cook."

Cook said, "Sure, sure," and hurried out; Sister followed him.

Adinda came back, picking fluff off her cardigan. "That bathroom is very smelly," she said, "and they have used all the paper."

Jan stood with his legs crossed and asked, in a strained voice, "Can you lift me?"

"Lift you?" Adinda asked, her eyebrows raised. "What on earth for?"

"Please, please," Jan said. "It hurts."

Suddenly there was a loud scraping noise and the ship shuddered. Steps pounded on the deck, but there were no voices. Adinda climbed nimbly into Jan's bunk and peered through the porthole.

They had arrived, and everything was white: the quay, the

coffins and the dead houses in the background. On the quayside stood a helicopter, its back and its huge propeller thick with snow; a small group of men stood near it with a stretcher. The two men in space suits were among them; the one with the sun glasses pointed his camera at the ship, the other lifted a reflector with a dead lamp in it.

Jan called, desperately, "Adinda, please!" but she didn't answer. She saw two people, stiff with snow, climb up the bank onto the quayside; they were Father Ambrosius and the farmer with the pitchfork. Father Ambrosius led the farmer by the hand; as they slowly walked toward the helicopter, Father Ambrosius started to nod again. Then, suddenly, there were two flashes of dazzling light; the farmer tore himself free, Father Ambrosius stumbled and fell in the snow, a voice shouted, "Hold him!" the farmer raised his pitchfork, and Adinda fell on the bunk, her face in her hands.

Voices shouted, steps thudded across the deck, doors slammed, then silence fell. But no one heeded Jan's plaintive cries, "Sister . . . Sister . . ." and he sat down, sobbing.

A door was opened, steps came along the corridor, Miss Winter's voice asked, "What's happened?" and Sparks' voice answered, hoarse with rage, "Those bloody photographers with their flashlights! They ought to be shot!"

"Miss Winter . . . Miss Winter . . ." Jan cried.

"But what happened?" Miss Winter's voice asked, shrilly, "for God's sake, what happened?"

"He stabbed the old priest with his pitchfork at least three times, before they could get hold of him," Sparks said. "The bastards, the bastards . . ."

Then Jan could hold out no longer. He screamed. "Miss Winter!" at the top of his voice; as she appeared in the doorway, white and trembling, he sobbed, "I've wet my pants, but I couldn't help it."

Miss Winter stared at him with horrified eyes; then she stammered, "You . . . you naughty boy," took him in her arms, and burst out weeping.

After the helicopter had taken off with a deafening roar, the children were put to bed, but they could not sleep. For one thing, it was too early, and then people kept coming in to get things out of the cupboard; Sister came in twice, then the doctor. Jan asked where Father was, but the doctor said, "Ssh! Go to sleep," and went away.

An hour later, fires were lit on the quayside. Jan got to his knees and looked out of the porthole. There were four fires, flickering red in the snow that had started to swirl again; men in duffel coats, the hoods over their heads, stood around them warming their hands. Then he heard the drone of an airplane approaching. It hovered in the sky for a long time; at last a helicopter came roaring down between the fires. Jan called, "Adinda! Adinda, look!" but she did not answer. The helicopter coming down was a wonderful sight; the draught of its huge thrashing propeller flattened the fires and whipped up a blizzard of snow; steam burst from the fires, and the shadows of the hooded men staggered in the clouds like giants. Then the propeller stopped, the fires became quiet again, the snow swirled once more, and out of the helicopter came two soldiers, who went to the ship.

After Jan had sat looking for a while at the snow gathering on the helicopter's propeller and back, he started to call for Sister. As no one came, he got out of his bunk, and sneaked down the passage. There was a strange light in the hospital; when he peered round the corner, he saw it was candlelight. It came from the bunk in the far left-hand corner, in which a still form was lying. A soldier with a white stole over his battledress knelt beside the bunk, chanting, a cross in his folded hands. At the foot of the bunk, the faces of Mr. Grijpma, Mr. Tadema and the doctor floated in the darkness of the dining room, faintly luminous in the candlelight.

As Jan stealthily crept nearer, there was a rustle of skirts, a hand grabbed his shoulder, and he was firmly led back to the nursery. "Now you stay in your bed, or I'll put the bars back," Sister whispered. She lifted him into his bunk, then she bent over Adinda. Jan heard her whisper, "What's the matter, girl? Why are you crying?" When she got no answer, she straightened up and went to the wash basin to get a glass of water. She rustled back, bent over Adinda again, and said, "Come on. Drink this." There was a silence, then she said, "All right. Have it your own way," and emptied the glass again into the wash basin. At the door, she whispered, "I won't put the bars back this time, but one more sound out of you and that's what I'll do."

After she had shut the door, Jan asked in a whisper, "Adinda? Adinda, what's the matter?" Then he lowered himself out of his bunk and got into hers. He put his arm around her and she put her head on his shoulder. He felt her face was wet. "What's the matter?" he whispered. "Have you got a pain?" She shook her head, and as he knew that she would not answer, he asked no more questions, but just lay there, his arm around her, listening to her uneven breathing until it slowly calmed down.

He was nearly asleep when the door was opened and two dark shapes entered. They did not put on the light, but they left the door open; he recognized Mr. Grijpma and Mr. Tadema. Mr. Grijpma was carrying his rolled-up mattress. He put it on the floor, sat down on it and started to unlace his shoes. Then, suddenly, he rested his head on his knee.

Mr. Tadema sat down beside him and whispered, "Would you like me to ask the doctor to give you a sleeping draught?"

Mr. Grijpma shook his head, without looking up.

"I would if I were you," Mr. Tadema whispered. "You are very tired, you haven't had a good rest since the flood, and now this. . . ."

"It isn't that," Mr. Grijpma said, huskily. "I'm all right."

Mr. Tadema put a hand on his shoulder and asked, "What is it? Tell me."

Mr. Grijpma shook his head again, and went on unlacing his shoes.

"I think the best thing for you to do," Mr. Tadema whispered, "would be to leave tomorrow, with your children. The waterboat is going to Rotterdam. If I were you, I'd go with it."

Mr. Grijpma rested his head on his knee again.

"You know," Mr. Tadema whispered, "I think our work is done. When those journalists said this morning that they would make inquiries about my flag, I knew the time for us to go was near. From now on, this is no longer an emergency but a mili-

[193]

tary operation. The professionals are taking over, and that young priest is one of them."

Mr. Grijpma put his hands in front of his face and Jan heard to his alarm that he was crying.

"I know exactly how you feel," Mr. Tadema whispered. "That's all I can say."

They sat for a long while like that, in silence; then Mr. Tadema whispered, "I'll go and get you that sleeping draught. Believe me, it's only sensible." He got to his feet and went away.

When he returned he was carrying a glass. He knelt beside Mr. Grijpma, held out his hand and said, "Here, take this." Mr. Grijpma wiped his eyes, took the pill and gulped it down with water, then he gave the glass back to Mr. Tadema and whispered hoarsely, "Thank you."

"Will you be all right now?" Mr. Tadema asked.

Mr. Grijpma nodded. "Quite all right," he whispered, "thank you very much."

Mr. Tadema patted his shoulder and went away, closing the door behind him. Jan heard Mr. Grijpma undress in the darkness, lie down on his mattress and sigh. He waited a long time, then he asked, "Father? May we come into bed with you?"

At first he thought that Mr. Grijpma had not heard, then his voice came from the darkness, very close. "Yes," he said.

Jan climbed out of the bunk without letting go of Adinda's hand. "Come," he whispered, "come on, Adinda." He felt her climb out after him, and he cautiously groped his way on all fours until he found Mr. Grijpma. He lay down beside him and put his head on his shoulder, then he felt Adinda crawl over them; she lay down on the other side.

"Have you been awake all the time?" Mr. Grijpma asked.

"Yes," said Jan. "We heard everything, and I saw the candles."

Mr. Grijpma said, "Ah."

"Is he dead?" Adinda's voice asked in the darkness.

Mr. Grijpma said, "Yes."

"Why did Sparks say, 'Those photographers ought to be shot'?" Jan asked. "He sounded very angry."

"He was mistaken," Mr. Grijpma said. "They took their photographs because they thought Father Ambrosius nodded his approval."

They lay for a while in silence, then Jan asked, "Are we going to leave tomorrow with the waterboat?"

Mr. Grijpma said, "Perhaps."

"Will we go to Rotterdam?"

"We may."

"And then? Where do we go then?"

Mr. Grijpma said, "Ssh. We'll see tomorrow."

They were silent again, and Jan was nearly asleep when he heard Adinda say, "Old Karto had a kris."

"What's that?" Mr. Grijpma asked, drowsily.

"A knife shaped like a snake," Adinda said. "It was poisoned."

Mr. Grijpma said, "Ssh. Sleep, my dear," and so they fell asleep.

Jan was woken up by sunlight, shining on his face. He got up, climbed on his bunk to look out of the porthole and was dazzled by the white world outside. The helicopter was gone, and so were the fires. Thick snow covered their traces. A trail of footprints led from the ship to the row of coffins opposite. As he sat gazing, a cart with dead cattle drove past, silently. Its wheels no longer rattled, and the hoofs of the horse thudded softly in the snow.

The ship was very quiet; Mr. Grijpma and Adinda were still asleep, their mouths open, their arms flung out. Adinda, as always when she was asleep, looked about three years old; Mr. Grijpma looked old and silly. Jan tiptoed to the door, opened it cautiously and peered out. He heard voices in the hospital and was about to step into the corridor, when the doctor came out of the bathroom.

"Your father awake?" he asked.

Jan shook his head.

"Don't come out," the doctor said, pushing him back into the room; then he put his head round the door. Mr. Grijpma lay blinking; the sunlight glistened in the stubble on his face. "Good morning, good morning," he said.

"I didn't want to wake you up," said the doctor, "but perhaps it's just as well. It has been decided with the priest that he'll be buried together with those unidentified children. They're getting him ready now; the funeral will be in an hour's time."

"I'll be ready," Mr. Grijpma said. "I'm getting up now."

"Don't hurry," said the doctor. "I'll have some breakfast brought in to you. I think it's better the children don't come out just yet."

"Splendid," Mr. Grijpma said. "Thank you very much. I'm getting up now."

He dressed hastily, while Adinda yawned and stretched, upsetting Ko who started to hop around, pretending he had a destination. Bussy yawned also, sticking up his hindquarters and stretching his front paws, and Jan, back on his bunk, put his arm across Noisette to see how far he could go. When she did not protest, he put his leg across her and she lay on her back, her eyes closed, ominously thrashing her tail. The cook popped in, carrying a tray with paper mugs and a plate of unappetizing sandwiches; he grinned, said, "Good morning! Glorious day, isn't it?" and popped out again.

When Mr. Grijpma was dressed, the children were still sprawling, and so were the animals, except Bussy who stood at the door wagging his tail, looking expectant. "Come on, children, hurry up!" Mr. Grijpma said. "We don't want to keep the people waiting."

"Who says Ko is a man?" Jan asked musingly, staring at Ko from the top bunk. Ko was sniffing up and down the paneling in the corner underneath the wash basin, his ears pricked up.

"Please, please, children," Mr. Grijpma said, old and flustered, "please get dressed and eat your breakfast. We've slept much too long."

"I had a lovely dream," said Adinda, her eyes closed, her legs spread, her hands under her head. "I dreamed I was walking along a long lane of palm trees with two white mice on leashes of gold thread."

Bussy, now looking as worried as Mr. Grijpma, crawled toward her, sniffed under her arm and yapped halfheartedly, wagging his tail.

Mr. Grijpma sat down on the lower bunk, bent forward in an uncomfortable position, and started to munch one of Cook's sandwiches hastily, as if he were waiting for a train. Jan dangled one leg out of the top bunk, swung it and said, "We never heard that helicopter leave."

Adinda said, "It was very warm and I felt the light and the shadow as I walked, hot and cool, and then, at the end of the lane . . ."

"Animal!" Mr. Grijpma cried. They all looked at Bussy, squatting underneath the wash basin.

[197]

"Good thing we're leaving," Adinda said, "About everybody has pee'd in this room by now, except me and Jesus."

Mr. Grijpma cried, "What?" lowering the sandwich he was raising to his mouth. "What did you say?"

Adinda closed her eyes and said, sullenly, "Nothing."

Mr. Grijpma suddenly got very tense and worked up. "I insist!" he cried, "I demand an answer! What did you say?"

Adinda, without opening her eyes, answered flatly, "Nothing. A hymn we used to sing at the Mission School."

"What hymn?" Mr. Grijpma asked, his knuckles white on the edge of the bunk.

"Just a hymn," Adinda said. "Nobody knows the trouble I've seen, except me and Jesus."

Mr. Grijpma said, miserably, "I see." He raised the sandwich to his mouth once more, thought better of it and put it back on the plate. "Listen, children," he said in a weary voice, "I know we're all tired and upset, and a bit dizzy perhaps because of the pill we have taken, but we must promise one another to be kind and lenient, whatever happens. I mean, we're leaving today, so don't let's spoil it all by getting angry."

The children looked at him warily. They had no idea what he was talking about, but they realized that the glorious holiday in which all grownups had loved them whatever they did or said was drawing to its close. Mr. Grijpma looked at them with a strange despair in his eyes. "All right," he said. "Now show that you have understood by getting dressed quickly."

They dressed in a glum silence, nurturing a secret feud at the wash basin. They didn't whisper, they didn't even nudge or pinch, they just exerted a secret pressure on one another as they stood brushing their teeth, but neither of them betrayed it. Adinda said, "Here's the towel, Jan," and Jan said, "Thank you,

Adinda," while in their minds they were pinching, kicking and spitting.

Mr. Grijpma, still munching his first mouthful of the cook's sandwich, said, "Let's dedicate this day to the memory of those who are asleep."

Adinda raised her eyebrows and stared at Jan with expressionless eyes; Jan turned purple, and the laugh came out of his nose. Adinda went to the mattress, got the dirty handkerchief from underneath the pillow, and handed it to Jan between her finger and thumb. Jan silently mouthed the word "Bloodsucker," and Adinda said sweetly, "Yes, dear, they're brushed very well."

"It's miraculous," Mr. Grijpma said, behind them. "There isn't a single situation in life that isn't formulated and resolved in the Bible." He was still sitting on the edge of the bunk, his dog-eared little Bible open in his hands. "Listen to this," he said. "Of the times and the seasons, brethren, ye have no need that I write unto you. For yourselves know perfectly that the day of the Lord so cometh as a thief in the night. For when they shall say, Peace and safety; then sudden destruction cometh upon them, as travail upon a woman with child; and they shall not escape."

Noisette arched her back above him, stretched, yawned and peered down at the top of his head.

"The only trouble is," Mr. Grijpma said, scratching his head as if he felt Noisette's stare, "that after those verses ought to follow the last six verses of the previous chapter. I wonder if I can do that. . . ."

Noisette jumped to the floor from the top bunk, minced toward Ko, who was inspecting the paneling, and sniffed at his tail. Ko kicked back like a mule, Noisette darted away.

"I think I will," Mr. Grijpma said, shutting the Bible. "It's all God's word. Are you ready, children?"

Adinda, who was pinning the medallion and the watch to her cardigan with the "Mother" brooch, said, "Just a minute."

Jan asked, "Why do you put on that silly watch? It has said half past twelve ever since you found it."

Adinda said, calmly, "That's none of your bloody business," at which Mr. Grijpma cried, "Children! I beseech you! Even if you can't feel compassion, show dignity!"

The children, without understanding what he meant, sensed the febrility of his self-control, finished dressing and followed him as he went to the dining room.

The hospital seemed very stuffy as they passed between the bunks; the patients were all awake but they just lay still and stared at them as they passed, without saying good morning or even smiling. The bunk in the far corner where the candles had been was empty. In the dining room the blacksmith, Sparks, the nurseryman and Mr. Tadema sat munching their bread and sipping their coffee. Mr. Grijpma said, "We've had our breakfast. Shall we wait outside?" Mr. Tadema shrugged his shoulders, then he nodded. Mr. Grijpma said, "Come on, children," helped them up the steps to the little hall, and they put on their coats and mufflers.

As they came out they saw on the aft deck, in front of the steering wheel, a coffin that looked bright and new because it was the only thing in sight not covered with snow. There were no clouds in the sky and there was no wind; as they stood looking around, a shower of snow fell off the row of coffins opposite and they heard the soft rustle in the distance.

"Well, children?" said Mr. Grijpma with a forced smile. "What if you went for a little walk up and down the quay, while I sit here and compose the text for the funeral?"

The children nodded. As Adinda went toward the gangplank, Jan nudged her and whispered, "I'll get Bussy." He slipped back inside; while he was away, Adinda watched Mr. Grijpma out of the corner of her eye, unbuttoning her coat and buttoning it again. He had sat down in the snow on the little platform behind the steering wheel and opened his Bible, but he wasn't reading. He just sat staring at the coffin through the spokes, looking old and sad.

Jan came back, carrying Bussy; they shuffled down the slippery gangplank and climbed the slope of the quay. When they were on top Jan put down Bussy, who sank up to his neck in the snow. They walked away; Jan called softly, "Bussy! Come on, boy!" Bussy tried to walk toward them; when he found that by doing so he buried himself in the snow, he yapped, jumped and rolled on his back. When he scrambled to his feet again he looked like a little Polar bear. The children laughed, careful not to make a sound, and Jan picked him up again. They ploughed through the thick snow until Mr. Grijpma was out of sight, then they put Bussy down again and started to make a snowman.

The funeral procession approached so silently that it was upon them before they realized it; a double file of sailors, each pair carrying a small coffin between them. They got hastily to their feet, Jan picked up Bussy and ran back to the gangplank as fast as he could. Mr. Grijpma didn't notice him; he stood staring at the small procession from behind the steering wheel, the Bible open in his hand. The procession came to a halt at the gangplank, the sailors put down their coffins and started to warm their hands by slapping their shoulders, their arms across their chests.

Mr. Tadema, the blacksmith, the nurseryman and Sparks came out on deck, stamping their feet to get their boots on; then they stooped, lifted the coffin onto their shoulders and carried it cautiously ashore. As they took up position at the head of the procession, the young soldier with the white stole over his battle-dress came hurrying out of one of the houses behind the wall of coffins, wiping his mouth with his sleeve. He took a cross out of his trouser pocket, lifted it in his folded hands, looked over his shoulder, nodded, and the sailors picked up their small coffins again. The procession started to move; Mr. Grijpma and the children followed. There were no civilians this time. They were the only mourners.

The walk to the dike was long and arduous because the snow was so thick. The hem of Adinda's skirt turned white as it trailed through the snow; Jan got so tired lifting his feet that he ended by taking big steps, putting his feet in the footprints left by the sailor in front of him. When at last they climbed the dike and looked out over the sea on either side, they saw in the distance, across the gray water, the thin white lines of the dikes of the other islands, broken in many places.

Yet it seemed as if the flood had not happened; all was still and peaceful. The vast white plain of wreckage that stretched out from the foot of the dike looked like a big ploughed field snowed under. The grave was white too, and the mound beside it looked smooth and shiny as if it had been there forever.

As Jan stood waiting at Mr. Grijpma's side, watching the coffins being lowered into the grave by the sailors, his feet began to get cold, and he hoped the service would not be long. He wriggled his toes inside his galoshes to warm them; then his nose got cold. He blew his breath upward to warm it, and saw it make little clouds of steam. They made him think of the UK 516, and the black rings blown by the pipe between its masts; he secretly tried to blow rings too.

"Of the times and the seasons, brethren," Mr. Grijpma read, in a hoarse, shaky voice, "ye have no need that I write unto you."

Jan saw that the big coffin was gone; the sailors stood to attention round the white grave, the ribbons on their caps moved in the gentle wind.

"For when they shall say, Peace and safety; then sudden destruction cometh upon them . . ." Mr. Grijpma croaked, his voice thin and strained in the vast white stillness, "and they shall not escape. But I would not have you to be ignorant, brethren, concerning them which are asleep, that ye sorrow not, as others which have no hope. For if we believe that Jesus died and rose again, even so them also which sleep in Jesus will God bring with Him. . . . For the Lord himself shall descend from heaven with a shout, with the voice of the archangel, and with the trump of God: and the dead in Christ shall rise first: Then we which are alive and remain shall be caught up together with them in the clouds, to meet the Lord in the air: and so shall we ever be with the Lord. Wherefore comfort one another with these words. Amen."

He had read it very badly; he shut his Bible and stepped back, his head bent. While the young soldier with the white stole took his place and started to chant in Latin, blessing the grave with the cross, tears ran down the gray stubble on his face, and Jan saw, out of the corner of his eye, Adinda take his hand. He took the other hand, and stood waiting for the young soldier to finish chanting, wriggling his toes.

When the soldier had finished, the sailors took their spades and started to spoil the smooth white mound. Jan saw with regret its beautiful slope change into a jagged black wound. The white grave was spoiled too; when they finally turned away to go back to the ship, they left behind them a dark patch with trampled mud around it.

On board, the cook had hot chocolate waiting. The patients were talking now; the man with the red beard was sitting up in his bunk, smoking a cigar. In the dining room, a stranger sat waiting for them, sipping cocoa. He had a peaked cap on, a dirty uniform jacket over a roll-necked jersey, and he too was unshaven. Mr. Tadema introduced him as the captain of the waterboat.

"Well, Parson," the captain said cheerfully, "all set for our leaving at high tide. I've tied up your houseboat. It's a perfect day for towing it to Rotterdam."

"But—but it isn't my houseboat," Mr. Grijpma stammered, "it isn't my houseboat at all!"

"Well," said the captain, "then whose is it?"

"Mrs. Ool's," Mr. Grijpma answered, "one of the members of my congregation."

"Well," said the captain, "where's Mrs. Ool?"

Mr. Grijpma shrugged his shoulders, and the captain said, "Well, whomever it may belong to, we're going to tow it to Rotterdam, on the lieutenant's orders. He says it's cluttering up the harbor."

So, that afternoon, they set out from Onderkerk in the waterboat. They sat on the bench in front of the wheelhouse, the animals on their laps, a rug over their knees. At their feet stood a basket, which a running sailor had delivered in the nick of time.

"Well, children," Mr. Grijpma said, when the ship had sailed into the open and they had sat staring at the sea and the broken white lines of the dikes for a while in silence, "this afternoon we'll be in Rotterdam. There we'll take a taxi to the station, and if we are lucky with the trains, we may be in Elburg tonight. The only trouble is, I haven't got any money; but I suppose somebody on the dry land will lend me some, if I tell him I'm a clergyman."

"Where's Elburg?" Jan asked.

"It's a little old town on the shores of the Zuider Zee," Mr. Grijpma answered, "where a dear friend of mine is parson. He doesn't know it yet, but I'm sure he'll be very happy to put us up for a month or so, until we go back."

"Back where?" Adinda asked. "There's nothing left to go back to."

"The dikes will be mended and the water pumped out," Mr. Grijpma said. "The islands will rise again from the sea, and if the old Niewerland is gone, we'll build a new one."

"How long will that take?" Adinda asked.

"I don't know," Mr. Grijpma answered. "Maybe many years. We'll have to live in little wooden huts at first, while they are building, but that doesn't matter as long as we are together."

"Will we take Bussy?" Jan asked.

"Of course," Mr. Grijpma said.

"And Ko and Noisette?"

"Of course."

"And Prince?"

Mr. Grijpma hesitated, then he answered, "And Prince."

"Why?" Jan asked. "Nobody likes him. You don't like him either. I know that. Why take him?"

"Well," said Mr. Grijpma, "it may not sound much of a reason, but I can't forget how much your mother loved him, and . . . well, he may calm down in the end."

"If Mother loved him so, why don't we kill him?" Jan asked. "He'll go up in the clouds and meet her in the air."

[205]

"Don't talk nonsense," Mr. Grijpma said.

"That's what you read this morning," Jan said, "about Father Ambrosius and the children. Why doesn't that go for Prince?"

Mr. Grijpma sighed; Ko, on his lap, opened his eyes, and pricked up his ears. "Well," Mr. Grijpma said, "I'll try to explain it to you. . . ."

He tried to explain it to him, while far ahead on the horizon sunlight flashed on the wings of the first windmill of the unharmed land.

Four months later, one warm morning in June, a monkey sat in the center of what once had been the village square of Niewerland, attached to a flagpole by a chain. He belonged to Captain Bas, water-builder in charge of reclamation, District Sixteen C. Captain Bas lived on board his own dredger, lying in the harbor: a huge floating factory of steel girders, conveyor belts, bucket ladders and cranes, with two gray funnels side by side, belching black smoke. Captain Bas wore a bowler hat and carpet slippers, his cabin had geraniums in front of the portholes, two parakeets in a cage, a spring-driven cuckoo clock and a pipe rack with the legend, "East, West, Home Is Best." He had come with his dredger from Hong Kong to reclaim the drowned land, and he had brought the monkey with him.

The monkey squatted with sad eyes in the sunlight, his hands on his knees, his head between his shoulders, and listened to a choir of shrill children's voices screaming, "Holland, Home of the Brave." The singing came from the open windows of a prefabricated wooden shack with a row of small mud boots in front, standing in the cleared center of a heap of rubble that had once been the village school. There was another shack nearby, with a row of big mud boots in front, standing on a patch cleared in the ruins of the old Town Hall. In fact, all that was left of the old village of Niewerland was the church, but it had been buttressed up with poles and planking to prevent its bulging walls sagging out still more.

The rest of the village had been pounded to rubble by the waves that had reigned supreme for over four months. It now looked like a rock garden: everywhere among the rubble, weeds and white onion flowers had emerged, and one of the dead tree trunks around the prehistoric barrow of the parsonage had miraculously sprouted two green twigs. The only place that was neat and tidy was the churchyard. The old tombstones had been washed clean; there were no weeds between them; the triple row of new graves had been neatly raked, and the wooden crosses at their heads painted white.

There were other prefabricated shacks, standing among the rubble. There was one where Hank the blacksmith's forge had been; one a little farther, with painted on its gable, "*F. Snop, Baker and Undertaker*"; one near the harbor, showing a big freshly painted sign with a yellow and green parrot saying, "*In the Drowned Parrot—Groceries*." Far away, at the bottom of the jagged rampart of the broken dike, on the edge of a tremendous mud flat that stretched out to the horizon, and that looked void and without form like the earth on the first day of its creation, was another little prefabricated shack, next to the ruin of Bouma's farm. Behind it a horse and a calf stood dumbly gazing at the gray emptiness; the only one quite at home was a fat, dirty pig, snorting and rolling in pig's paradise.

The center of activity was the harbor. Around Captain Bas' gigantic dredger lay a fleet of lighters, floating cranes, mud scows, sand scoopers and caisson vessels; on the dike, a long row of barracks had been erected to house the families of the water-builders that were to reclaim the land. The choir of little scream-ers yelling in the schoolhouse was composed of the water-builders' children, all of whom spoke two languages: either Dutch and Gaelic, or Dutch and Turkish, or Dutch and Urdu, depending on where their fathers had been posted of late.

As the monkey sat sadly staring at the rubble, the onion flowers and the fat white clouds slowly sailing overhead, there came from the sea the squeak of a hooter and a small convoy moved into the harbor. It consisted of an old tugboat with a high red funnel, wearing a white plume of steam, towing a dredger and behind it, skating nervously, a little houseboat painted white and green. When the convoy had entered the harbor, the dredger cast off first and moored alongside Captain Bas' factory; then the tugboat, puffing and snorting, sailed round the little houseboat, put its nose to its stern and pushed it into the dead end of the harbor.

A water-builder in a rowboat took care of its moorings; when it was safely tied up alongside the new jetty, its front door was opened and a gangplank put out. Along the gangplank came an old man in clerical garb, who wobbled across, his arms spread, as if he were walking a tightrope; he shook the water-builder by the hand, then he put on his spectacles and looked around. After him followed two children, who walked the plank side-ways, hand in hand, and stood looking round at the devastation with their mouths open. Then came a fair-sized dog, who walked

[209]

the plank clumsily and slipped at the end, so he landed hanging by his front paws; the children pulled him up. Then came six kittens, followed by a cat with a broken tail, who had no trouble with the gangplank at all. Then a little rabbit tried to hop toward the shore, slipped, and scurried back to join its mother and its nine brothers and sisters, who sat looking at the shore from the doorway. Then a trumpeting clarion call sounded; the rabbits scurried indoors, the cat and the kittens ran off toward the village square with their tails in the air, and onto the gangplank jumped a cock, as big as a goose. He stretched out his neck, bugled once more, scrambled precariously along the plank, jumped ashore and started to strut around, scratching.

The old man took the children by the hand, and they walked slowly along the mud tracks among the rubble toward the churchyard, picking onion flowers on their way. The dog, the cat and the kittens followed them. In the churchyard, they walked along the rows of new graves, reading the names on the crosses; they stopped at one of them, and the children put their bunches of onion flowers at the foot of the small mound. They stood looking at the grave for a while; the dog sat beside them, and the kittens sniffed cautiously at the bottoms of the crosses on the other graves. Then they walked away, to the shop of F. Snop, Baker and Undertaker. A man in floury overalls came out; he lifted the children and kissed them, and he shook the old man warmly by the hand.

During all this, the rabbits had settled down in the sun in the doorway of the houseboat, huddled close together, their eyes closed, and the cock had scratched and pecked his way to the village square, with an occasional bugle call of pride and self-assurance. The monkey, motionless, sat watching him out of the corner of his sad eyes, his hands on his knees, his head between his shoulders.

The doors of the school burst open, and let out a flock of cheering and dancing children. They ran to the square, swinging their satchels, plaits and ribbons flying, and clustered around the monkey, who got to his feet and started bowing, taking off an imaginary hat. He was given sweets, bits of bread and balls of paper; he sat down to munch the sweets and the bread; the balls of paper he stuck underneath his bald rump without as much as sniffing at them. The children ran on toward the row of shacks on the dike, skipping and shouting; a little girl lagged behind because her garter had come loose, and the cock flew at her, hissing. She screamed and ran, stumbling; the cock gave a clarion call of triumph, and resumed his scratching and pecking.

The monkey lifted a buttock, took a ball of paper from underneath and threw it at the cock with a gesture of lassitude. The cock strutted toward it, pecked, shook it and dropped it again, disgusted. He was still outside the faint circle of footprints surrounding the flagpole. The monkey threw another paper ball, within the circle; but the cock, after glancing at it with one beady eye, went on scratching and pecking, ignoring it.

That afternoon, the children from the houseboat joined the others, reluctantly shuffling to school. They were carrying brand new satchels and the girl had a fresh pink bow on top of her head. After they had vanished inside, the day became hotter, and the village became still. A woman from one of the shacks on the dike went to the houseboat, opened its windows and started hanging bedclothes and carpets out of them; and its chimney began to smoke.

Toward sundown, the school doors opened and the children

came dancing out again. They all formed a ring round the monkey, who again started bowing and taking off his imaginary hat. Then Captain Bas came ambling down from the harbor in his carpet slippers, smoking a pipe, his bowler hat over his eyes, his hands behind his back. He loosened the chain, took the monkey by the hand and walked back with him to his dredger. The monkey jumped up and down, waved his free arm at the children and pulled faces at them, but Captain Bas never looked round, as if he had not noticed any children.

Evening came, large and blue; as the sky darkened, and the last red clouds sailed into the night at the horizon, little lights sprang up everywhere: behind the windows of the prefabricated houses, the shacks on the dike, the houseboat and the little hut where Bouma's farm had been. On board Captain Bas' dredger, the lights stayed on all night; when silence and darkness had settled over the land there came, from the cabin with the geraniums behind the portholes, the mournful sounds of a trombone.

The next morning, as the sun rose over the misty land that looked young and asleep, the two children came out of the little houseboat and ran to the church with the dog galloping around them, barking. They vanished in the tower; a few minutes later the joyous sounds of bells rang out from the belfry. From the wooden houses, the shacks on the dike and the ships in the harbor, came men and women in black, carrying hymnbooks, who stolidly trod their way toward the church. From an arch in the belfry, the heads of the children and the dog watched them as they came.

When everybody had gone inside, the village was empty, except for the monkey squatting in the square at the end of his chain, and the cock scratching and pecking around him. From the church came the mournful sound of a trombone, that started to drag the singsong of the congregation through a long, slow psalm. While they were singing, and while the children sat gazing over the land from the arch of the belfry, the cock stepped inside the faint circle of footprints, stretched his neck and started his clarion call. But he never finished it, for with a flash that was quicker than the eye could see, the monkey had pounced upon him, and plucked him with the speed of a lawnmower.

One second later, a stark naked bird ran crazily toward the houseboat, screeching; and from the belfry, over the vast waste of the reborn land, sounded the thin cheering of children.